Celebrating WildGame

Members' Special Recipes

MINNETONKA, MINNESOTA

Celebrating Wild Game

MEMBERS' SPECIAL RECIPES

Celebrating Wild Game: Members' Special Recipes

The North American Hunting Club proudly presents this special edition cookbook that includes the personal favorites of your fellow Members. Each recipe has been screened by a cooking professional and edited for clarity. However, we are not able to kitchen-test these recipes and cannot guarantee their outcome or your safety in their preparation or consumption. Please be advised that any recipes that require the use of dangerous equipment (such as pressure cookers) or potentially unsafe procedures (such as marinating, canning or pickling) should be used with caution and safe, healthy practices.

Mike Vail
Vice President, Product and Business Development

Tom Carpenter
Director of Book and New Media Development

Dan Kennedy
Book Production Manager

Heather Koshiol
Book Development Coordinator

Matt Preis
Book Development Assistant

Beowulf
Book Design and Production

PHOTOGRAPHY

Phil Aarrestad	*Commissioned Photography*
Abigail Wyckoff	*Prop & Food Stylist*
Susan Telleen	*Assistant Food Stylist*
John Keenan	*Assistant Photographer*

Thanks to: Jeff Hedtke Sporting Collections; Mark Braaten Moose Calls; Bigstone Hunt Club: Mike Finch; Kent Montgomery; Ben and Mark Norquist; Mac Farlane Pheasant Farm; Native Game; Shaffer Farms.

1 2 3 4 5 6 7 8 / 02 01 00 99

ISBN 1-58159-056-3
North American Hunting Club
12301 Whitewater Drive
Minnetonka, MN 55343

Table of Contents

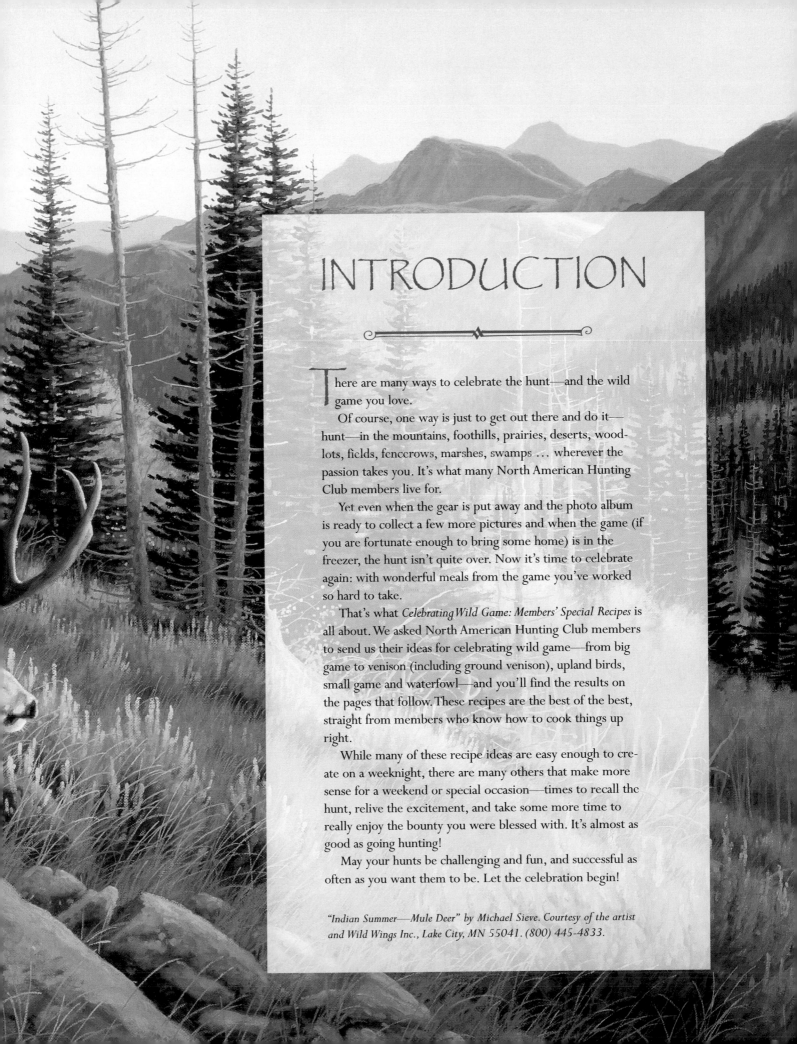

INTRODUCTION

There are many ways to celebrate the hunt—and the wild game you love.

Of course, one way is just to get out there and do it—hunt—in the mountains, foothills, prairies, deserts, woodlots, fields, fencerows, marshes, swamps … wherever the passion takes you. It's what many North American Hunting Club members live for.

Yet even when the gear is put away and the photo album is ready to collect a few more pictures and when the game (if you are fortunate enough to bring some home) is in the freezer, the hunt isn't quite over. Now it's time to celebrate again: with wonderful meals from the game you've worked so hard to take.

That's what *Celebrating Wild Game: Members' Special Recipes* is all about. We asked North American Hunting Club members to send us their ideas for celebrating wild game—from big game to venison (including ground venison), upland birds, small game and waterfowl—and you'll find the results on the pages that follow. These recipes are the best of the best, straight from members who know how to cook things up right.

While many of these recipe ideas are easy enough to create on a weeknight, there are many others that make more sense for a weekend or special occasion—times to recall the hunt, relive the excitement, and take some more time to really enjoy the bounty you were blessed with. It's almost as good as going hunting!

May your hunts be challenging and fun, and successful as often as you want them to be. Let the celebration begin!

"Indian Summer—Mule Deer" by Michael Sieve. Courtesy of the artist and Wild Wings Inc., Lake City, MN 55041. (800) 445-4833.

CHAPTER 1

BIG GAME

◦───✦───◦

Take a bite of elk, antelope, moose or any other big game, and you're getting more than just meat. You're also tasting the country it came from—celebrating the anticipation and work it took you to get there, harvest the game, pack it out and bring it all the way to your table. And sometimes, right in camp, you'll have the opportunity to eat some of the game while you're still "out there," under the stars. This is another very special celebration.

No matter what the occasion, the big game you have harvested is worthy of a celebration. Here are the ideas you need to plan it right.

"A Challenge to All—World Record Elk" by Ron Van Gilder.
Courtesy of the artist and Wild Wings Inc., Lake City, MN 55041.
(800) 445-4833.

ELK BOURGUIGNONNE

3 to 4 lbs. boneless elk stew meat, cut into cubes
Cooking oil
2/3 cup sliced carrots
2 cups sliced onion
3 cups quartered mushrooms
1 bottle red wine
Enough beef stock or broth to bring wine to 5 to 6 cups
2 to 3 large unpeeled cloves garlic, crushed
2 cups chopped tomatoes
1 bay leaf
1 tsp. thyme
1 tsp. salt
1/2 cup flour or cornstarch
2 T. softened butter

Thoroughly dry meat (elk, venison or lamb) with paper towels. Oil skillet and place on medium high heat. When skillet is hot but not smoking, brown meat in batches, adding oil as needed. Transfer browned meat to large pot. Sauté carrots 4 to 5 minutes until brown; add to meat. Sauté onion until soft and starting to brown. Add mushrooms and continue to sauté until mushrooms are softened; set onion and mushrooms aside. Deglaze browning skillet with 1/2 cup wine; add wine to meat. Add beef stock and remaining wine to meat. Add garlic, tomatoes, bay leaf, thyme and salt. Liquid should barely cover meat. Simmer assembled ingredients for 2 1/2 to 3 hours on low heat, turning meat periodically until fork tender. If preferred, place ingredients in casserole and bake at 425°F for 10 to 15 minutes; reduce heat to 350°F and cook for 2 1/2 to 3 hours.

When meat is tender, pour cooked ingredients through colander over large saucepan. Remove meat to pot or casserole. Press contents of colander to strain liquid; reserve liquid and discard strained ingredients. Make paste of flour or cornstarch and softened butter; thicken juices in saucepan with paste. Boil down to about 3 cups to concentrate flavor. Return sauce to meat and add sautéed onions and mushrooms. Heat through for about 5 minutes. Serve over large noodles or with mashed potatoes and boiled and buttered carrots or parsnips. Can be made several days ahead and reheated.

Peter Van Hauer
Golden Valley, MN

BIG GAME

CORNED BIG GAME

8-10 lbs. moose, elk, bear or other big game
1¹⁄₂ cups pickling salt
¹⁄₂ cup sugar
1 T. pickling spice
1 tsp. whole cloves
1 tsp. peppercorns
3 bay leaves
1¹⁄₂ tsp. saltpeter
7 qts. warm water
1 T. minced onion
2 cloves garlic, minced

In large glass, crockery or stainless steel container, mix all ingredients but meat until salt and sugar are dissolved. Add meat and press with weight if necessary to keep meat submerged. Cover and refrigerate for 15 days, turning meat and stirring and skimming brine every other day. To store, refrigerate meat with brine in zippered freezer bag; do not freeze. May be canned.

PASTRAMI

4 lbs. corned meat (corned as above)
1 T. pickling spice
2 cloves garlic
1 T. cracked peppercorns
¹⁄₂ tsp. allspice
¹⁄₂ tsp. paprika
¹⁄₂ tsp. nutmeg

Remove meat from brine, wash, cover with cold water and cook until ²⁄₃ done. Dry and press spices into meat. Smoke until internal temperature reads 160°F.

CHIPPED CORNED MEAT

Corned muscle cut (corned as above). Remove meat from brine, wash, dry and hang in cool place to air-dry for 24 hours. Cool-smoke at 100° to 200°F for 70 to 80 hours or until meat is quite dry. If necessary to avoid freezing, bring meat in at night and resume smoking during the day. Slice the meat very thin. May be refrigerated, canned or vacuum packed.

Andi Flanagan
Seward, AK

Moose Hoagies

Moose steak
Oil
Black pepper
Onion, sliced
Green pepper, sliced
Garlic powder
Soy sauce

Remove silver skin and connecting tissue from moose and slice meat into thin strips. Brown with black pepper in oil. Add onion, green pepper, garlic powder and a dash of soy sauce. Cook until done. Serve on hoagie buns with hot or mild pepper rings, steak sauce or spicy mustard.

Mike Costello
Birch Run, MI

Wild Game San Marco

1 to 1¹/₂ lbs. moose, elk or venison steaks, cut
    into serving pieces
Meat tenderizer (optional)
1 envelope onion soup mix
16-oz. can diced tomatoes in juice
1 tsp. oregano
Salt and pepper
Garlic powder
2 T. olive oil
1 T. red wine vinegar

Arrange meat in large skillet and sprinkle with meat tenderizer if desired. Cover with soup mix and tomatoes. Sprinkle with oregano, salt, pepper, a generous amount of garlic powder, olive oil and red wine vinegar. Cover and simmer for 1 hour. Serve over rice or boiled potatoes.

Mary Anne Lecce
Collinsville, IL

BIG GAME

HUNTER'S CHILI

3 lbs. ground big game
¹/2 lb. bacon, chopped
3 medium onions, chopped
3 medium green peppers, chopped
¹/2 cup chopped celery
4 cloves garlic, minced
2 cans stewed tomatoes
2 T. dried parsley flakes
2 T. chili powder
1 tsp. salt
1 T. black pepper
2 cans kidney beans, undrained
1 can pinto beans in molasses, undrained

In Dutch oven, brown meat over medium heat, stirring occasionally. Remove from heat and set aside. Cook chopped bacon and add to browned meat, reserving bacon grease. Sauté onions, green peppers, celery and garlic in bacon grease until tender. Add tomatoes, parsley, chili powder, salt and pepper to Dutch oven. Heat to boiling, cover and reduce heat. Simmer for 1 hour to blend flavors. Stir in kidney and pinto beans and cook uncovered for 30 minutes. Serve with garlic toast.

James Scheffelmaier
Airdrie, Alberta

MEATBALL PARTY FAVORITES

1 lb. ground moose or venison
1 cup bread crumbs
1 egg, beaten
2 T. finely chopped onion
2 T. milk
1 clove garlic
1 tsp. salt
Pepper
1 T. vegetable oil
10-oz. jar red currant jelly
1 bottle chili sauce

Combine meat, bread crumbs, egg, onion, milk, garlic, salt and pepper and mix well. Shape into 1-inch meatballs and brown in oil. Lightly stir red currant jelly into chili sauce and pour over meatballs. Cover and simmer for 10 minutes until cooked through, basting meatballs occasionally. Serve with toothpicks.

Jeffrey Pinkerton
Bangor, ME

BIG GAME

CARIBOU STEW

2 lbs. caribou stew meat
3 T. flour
2 T. garlic powder
1 tsp. salt
1 tsp. pepper
2 cups boiling water
2 T. Worcestershire
16-oz. can stewed tomatoes
1 cup sliced carrots
1 large onion, chopped
3 medium potatoes, diced
1 cup chopped celery
1 can sweet corn
1 can green beans
Fresh parsley
$^1/_2$ tsp. Kitchen Bouquet
Water
Cornstarch or flour

Combine flour with garlic powder, salt and pepper in a plastic bag, add meat and shake to coat. Brown meat then add boiling water and Worcestershire sauce. Cook on low heat for 2 hours or until tender. Add tomatoes, carrots, onion, potatoes, celery, corn, green beans and parsley. Cook until vegetables are tender. Add Kitchen Bouquet and thicken with a mixture of water and cornstarch or flour.

L.C. Forslund
Warren, MN

BIG GAME

WILD GAME CRÊPES
WITH BLUE CHEESE AND WILD MUSHROOM SAUCE

1 lb. ground moose, caribou, elk or venison
2 cloves garlic, minced
1 small onion, chopped
1 egg
^{1}/3 cup blue cheese, crumbled
1 cup sour cream
Small can sliced black olives
Salt and pepper

CRÊPES
2 eggs
2 T. melted butter or salad oil
1^1/3 cups milk
1 cup flour
^{1}/2 tsp. salt

WILD MUSHROOM SAUCE
2 cups mixed sliced wild mushrooms
*   (hedgehog, chanterelle, etc.)*
2 T. butter
2 T. flour
^{3}/4 cup beef broth
^{1}/4 cup Madeira wine
^{3}/4 cup heavy cream
Freshly ground pepper

Brown venison, garlic and onion. Mix egg and cheese together and add to meat. Add sour cream and olives. Simmer for 5 minutes, stirring constantly. Season with salt and pepper (use salt sparingly as blue cheese can be quite salty). Cool mixture and fill 16 crêpes. Roll up and place in 13 x 9-inch pan. Cover with mushroom sauce and bake at 375°F for 20 minutes. Crêpes can also be frozen and baked for 30 minutes. Serve with spinach and bacon salad.

To make crêpes: Place ingredients in blender in order listed and blend at high speed for 30 seconds. Using 3 tablespoons of batter for each crêpe, make thin pancakes, turning when nearly dry on top. Cook only for a few seconds on flip side. Stack until ready to use.

To make sauce: Sauté mushrooms in butter. Add flour and stir for 2 minutes. Add beef broth, wine, cream and pepper. Simmer (do not boil) for 2 minutes. Serve sauce over wild game crêpes.

Andi Flanagan
Seward, AK

BIG GAME

BEAR SAUSAGE

5 lbs. bear meat
1 qt. buttermilk
1¹/₂ lbs. beef fat
2 T. Morton's Tender Quick or meat tenderizer
6 cloves garlic, crushed
2 tsp. ground black pepper
2 T. chervil
1 T. mustard seed
1 tsp. ground mustard
1¹/₂ T. ground sage
¹/₂ tsp. cayenne pepper
2 tsp. Worcestershire sauce
¹/₂ cup fine red wine
1 bunch cilantro, chopped
Sausage casing

Soak bear meat in buttermilk for 24 hours in refrigerator, stirring occasionally. Remove bear from marinade and grind both bear meat and beef fat. Add tenderizer, garlic, pepper, chervil, mustard seed, ground mustard, sage, cayenne pepper, Worcestershire suace, wine and cilantro to ground meat and fat and mix thoroughly. Stuff mixture into sausage casings and refrigerate until ready to grill.

Ron North
San Clemente, CA

South Texas
Wild Hog Meatballs

1-lb. pkg. ground wild hog sausage
1 slice white bread
1/3 cup milk
2 T. minced onion
2 T. chopped parsley
1 egg
1 1/2 T. extra virgin olive oil
6 T. freshly grated Parmesan cheese
1 whole nutmeg
Salt and freshly ground pepper
Fine, unflavored dried bread crumbs
Vegetable oil
Chili pepper seasoning (optional)

Trim crust from bread and heat bread and milk in small saucepan on low heat. When bread has completely soaked up milk, mash into pulp with fork and allow to cook. Combine meat, onion, parsley, egg, olive oil and grated Parmesan cheese in large bowl and mix thoroughly. Add a small grating of nutmeg (about 1/8 tsp.) and mix lightly.

Refrigerate for 30 minutes. Remove mixture from refrigerator and add bread mash, salt, several grindings of black pepper and pinch of chili pepper seasoning if desired. Gently knead mixture with hands without squeezing it. Form into 1-inch meatballs and roll lightly in bread crumbs. Refrigerate until cool. Pour 1/4 inch vegetable oil in pan and turn heat to medium. When oil is hot, gently place meatballs in skillet in single layer. Brown on all sides, being careful as you turn them. Serve as an appetizer dipped in Italian tomato sauce or honey-mix variety of barbecue sauce, or serve with Italian sauce over pasta.

Terry McCullough
Dallas, TX

STEVE'S BEAR STEW

3 lbs. bear stew meat
1 bottle regular or hickory marinade
2 lbs. small red potatoes, quartered
1 pkg. celery, sliced
1 lb. baby carrots, peeled
1 24-oz. pkg. small whole mushrooms
2 pkgs. onion gravy mix
16-oz. pkg. frozen peas
2 large onions, thinly sliced
2 tsp. Worcestershire sauce
$^1/_2$ tsp. thyme
$^1/_2$ tsp. salt
1 T. bacon bits
2 tsp. crushed garlic
2 beef bouillon cubes, dissolved in $^1/_2$ cup water
1 cup Madeira or red wine

Marinate meat 24 to 36 hours in marinade. When ready to cook, boil potatoes until half cooked. Drain potatoes and place in a 5-quart slow cooker. Combine celery, carrots, mushrooms, onion gravy mix, peas, onions, Worcestershire sauce, thyme, salt, bacon bits, garlic and bouillon. Mix well and cook on low setting for about 12 hours. Add wine and cook for another 2 hours.

Stephen Gingras
Lowell, MA

BURGUNDY WINE BEAR ROAST

2-lb. bear roast
4 to 5 medium potatoes, cut into chunks
6 carrots, cut into 2-inch chunks
2 onions, quartered
1 cup Burgundy wine
$^1/_2$ pkg. onion soup mix

Place meat, potatoes, carrots and onions in suitable baking dish. Mix soup and wine together and pour over meat and vegetables. Bake at 360°F for 1$^1/_2$ hours.

Kenneth W. Crummett
Sugar Grove, WV

SAUERKRAUT MOOSE BALLS

1 lb. ground moose

1/2 lb. ground pork

3 eggs

1 cup sauerkraut, squeezed dry and
    finely chopped

1/2 cup processed cheese spread

1 small onion, minced

1 tsp. minced garlic

Salt and pepper

1 cup dried fine bread crumbs

Oil for deep frying

Mix together all ingredients except bread crumbs. Roll into 1-inch balls, then in bread crumbs. Place on cookie sheet and chill 30 minutes. Heat oil to 400°F and deep fry balls a few at a time for about 30 seconds or until golden brown. Drain on paper towels. Serve with super hot or sweet hot mustard.

Andi Flanagan
Seward, AK

MOOSE POT PIE

1 lb. moose round steak

2 T. olive oil

4 T. lard

1 large onion, chopped

1 carrot, chopped

8 fresh mushrooms, sliced

1 large potato, diced

1 chili pepper, chopped

1 clove garlic, chopped

1/8 tsp. ground clove

1/8 tsp. nutmeg

1 tsp. salt

1/2 tsp. black pepper

1/2 tsp. sage

1 T. chervil or parsley

Two-crust pie shell

Cut round steak into 3/4-inch cubes. Heat oil and lard in large skillet. Sauté onion for 3 to 4 minutes. Add carrot, mushrooms, potato and chili pepper, cooking for 5 or 6 minutes before adding meat. As meat cooks, add garlic, clove, nutmeg, salt, pepper, sage and chervil or parsley. Add 1/4 cup water as needed. When potatoes are tender, remove skillet from heat and allow meat mixture to cool. Prepare bottom pie crust, fill with meat mixture and cover with top crust. Sprinkle top with freshly ground pepper. Bake at 400°F for 45 to 50 minutes. Serve hot.

Ron North
San Clemente, CA

WILD GAME SCALOPPINE MARSALA

1 lb. elk, moose or venison fillets
Meat tenderizer (optional)
Salt and pepper
1 egg
3 T. milk
²/3 cup seasoned bread crumbs
2 T. Parmesan cheese
4 T. butter, divided
1 T. chopped garlic
8 oz. fresh mushrooms, sliced
¹/2 cup thinly sliced green pepper
1 beef bouillon cube
1 cup water
2 tsp. flour
¹/4 to ¹/2 cup Marsala wine

Slice fillets horizontally into ¹/4-inch-thick strips. Season with salt and pepper and meat tenderizer if desired. Puncture meat lightly with a fork. Mix egg, milk, salt and pepper in a shallow bowl. Combine bread crumbs and Parmesan cheese in shallow bowl. Dip fillets in egg mixture, then coat with bread crumb mixture. Brown fillets in 2 T. butter and garlic, turning until lightly browned. Transfer to heated platter and keep warm. Sauté mushrooms and green pepper in remaining butter until tender. Dissolve bouillon cube in water. Add flour and mix well. Add this mixture and wine to mushrooms and green peppers, simmering on low until thickened. Serve over meat with wide noodles or wild rice.

   Variation: Substitute white wine and a splash of cognac (up to ³/4 cup) for Marsala. Add 1 diced fresh tomato, peeled and seeded, to mushrooms and substitute ¹/2 cup chopped canned artichoke hearts for green pepper.

Mary Anne Lecce
Collinsville, IL

MOOSE STEW

1 to 2 lbs. moose meat, cubed
1 can carrots, undrained
1 can peas, undrained
1 can corn, undrained
2 large potatoes, diced
1 large onion, diced
1 can beef soup
1 can minestrone soup
1 can beef gravy with mushrooms
3 bay leaves, crushed
Thyme
Basil

Sear moose cubes and keep juices. Combine meat and juices with carrots, peas, corn, potatoes and onion in large pot. Cook for 30 minutes. Add soups, gravy and your favorite seasonings (such as thyme and basil) and cook on low heat for 1½ to 2 hours.

Angel Roche
Miami, FL

ELK IN CIDER

3 lbs. boneless elk roast
3 cups apple cider (or more as needed)
1 T. whole peppercorns
1 T. whole cloves
1 T. celery seed
1 T. whole or ½ tsp. ground allspice
½ tsp. dry mustard
3 bay leaves
1 T. oil
1 large onion, chopped

Place meat in glass or ceramic bowl and add enough cider to cover. Add peppercorns, cloves, celery seed, allspice, dry mustard and bay leaves. Refrigerate overnight, turning meat occasionally in marinade. Lift meat out and wipe off any clinging spices. Strain and reserve marinade. Heat oil in Dutch oven and brown meat on all sides, adding onion halfway through. Pour in enough of marinade to come to 2 inches. Cover and simmer for 3 hours or until meat is tender.

Serve with sweet potatoes cooked in the juices, and hot, buttered greens.

Andi Flanagan
Seward, AK

WILD GAME COCKTAIL MEATBALLS

3 lbs. ground moose, elk, caribou or venison
4 slices white bread
1 cup milk
1 T. garlic powder
1 1/2 T. seasoned salt
3/4 T. pepper
4 T. minced onion flakes
1 T. oregano
1 T. paprika
1/2 tsp. cinnamon
3 eggs

SAUCE

1/4 cup butter
2 medium onions, very finely chopped
1/4 cup flour
3 cups beef broth
1 cup red wine
1/4 cup brown sugar
1/4 cup ketchup
2 T. lemon juice
6 to 8 ginger snaps, finely crumbled
2 tsp. salt
2 tsp. pepper

Tear bread into pieces and cover with milk in large bowl. Add remaining meatball ingredients and mix thoroughly. Shape into 1-inch balls. Place on jelly roll pan and bake at 330°F for 20 minutes.

For sauce, sauté chopped onions in butter until soft. Blend in flour. Add broth and stir until smooth. Add remaining sauce ingredients and stir. Add cooked meatballs and simmer for 10 to 15 minutes. Refrigerate for 12 to 24 hours. Reheat before serving.

Mary Anne Lecce
Collinsville, IL

Oriental Wild Game

1 1/2 *lbs. moose, elk or venison, thinly sliced on the diagonal*
1 jalapeño pepper, finely diced
1 medium onion, sliced vertically
1 medium zucchini, thinly sliced
1/2 lb. fresh mushrooms, quartered
Small can sliced water chestnuts (optional)
2 T. cornstarch
1/4 cup dry white wine

Marinade

1/3 cup teriyaki marinade and sauce
1/4 cup soy sauce
1 T. chopped garlic
1 tsp. Italian herbs, crumbled
1 tsp. ground ginger
1/2 tsp. cayenne pepper
1 tsp. seasoned salt
1 tsp. seasoned pepper
1 tsp. ground mustard
1 tsp. olive oil

Combine all marinade ingredients and marinate meat overnight in glass or ceramic container. Spray wok or large skillet with cooking oil spray. Cook meat, jalapeño, onion, zucchini and marinade for 10 to 15 minutes or until meat is browned and vegetables are tender. Add mushrooms and simmer for 5 minutes. Add water chestnuts if desired. Mix cornstarch and white wine until smooth and add to wok or skillet. Simmer until thickened. Serve over noodles or rice.

Mary Anne Lecce
Collinsville, IL

BIG GAME

Braised Sheep Chop Dinner

3 lbs. sheep chops
4 T. butter
1 onion, chopped
2 cloves garlic, chopped
3 potatoes, diced
2 ribs celery, chopped
1 turnip, diced
1 parsnip, sliced
2 carrots, sliced

Brown chops in butter in large skillet. Transfer meat to Dutch oven. Using butter remaining in skillet, brown onion and garlic and add to chops. Add potatoes, celery, turnip, parsnip and carrots to Dutch oven. Cover and roast at 300°F for 3 hours without removing lid. Serve with green beans in mustard sauce.

Andi Flanagan
Seward, AK

Summer Sausage

2 lbs. ground elk or venison (can substitute
  ground beef for $^1/_3$ of meat)
$^1/_4$ tsp. red pepper
$^1/_2$ tsp. black pepper
1 tsp. mustard seed
1 tsp. minced garlic or $^1/_4$ tsp. garlic powder
1 tsp. liquid smoke flavoring
2 T. Morton's Tender Quick or meat tenderizer
$^1/_4$ tsp. cracked black pepper

Mix all ingredients thoroughly. Mold into 3 or 4 logs and wrap in foil, twisting and folding over ends of foil. Refrigerate for 12 to 24 hours. Drop wrapped logs into large pot of boiling water and boil for 1 hour (or longer for double batch). Remove rolls, unwrap, drain and cool. When cool, rewrap and refrigerate for up to 7 to 10 days or freeze.

Jerry and Hope Brensinger
Mountain Home, ID

ELK PARMESAN

1¹/2 lbs. boneless elk steak
¹/4 to ¹/2 tsp. garlic powder
¹/2 tsp. salt
¹/8 tsp. pepper
¹/2 cup dry Italian bread crumbs
¹/2 cup grated Parmesan cheese
2 eggs
¹/4 cup water
¹/2 cup flour
¹/4 cup olive or vegetable oil
1¹/2 cups spaghetti sauce
6 slices mozzarella cheese

Cut meat into 6 pieces and pound with meat mallet to tenderize. Sprinkle with garlic powder, salt and pepper. Combine bread crumbs and Parmesan cheese in a bowl. In another bowl, beat eggs with water. Dip both sides of meat into flour, then egg mixture, then crumb mixture. Refrigerate steaks for 20 minutes. Heat oil in a large skillet and brown meat on both sides. Place steaks in a greased 9 x 13-inch pan. Spoon 2 tablespoons spaghetti sauce over each piece. Cover with mozzarella cheese and remaining sauce. Bake uncovered at 350°F for 30 minutes. Serve over cooked noodles.

Jerry and Hope Brensinger
Mountain Home, ID

MARINATED BEAR STEAKS

Bear steaks
2 cups buttermilk
1 tsp. ginger
2 cloves garlic, crushed
1 tsp. salt
1 tsp. pepper

Mix buttermilk, ginger, garlic, salt and pepper in nonaluminum bowl. Place bear steaks in marinade, cover and refrigerate for 24 hours, turning meat 2 or 3 times. Transfer steaks directly from marinade to hot grill and cook until well done.

Ron North
San Clemente, CA

BIG GAME

WILD GAME BOURGUIGNONNE

1¹/2 to 2 lbs. elk, moose or venison, cubed
Salt and pepper
Meat tenderizer (optional)
2 T. olive oil
1 T. chopped garlic
1¹/2 cups chopped onion or 6 oz. pearl onions
4 cups beef bouillon
1 T. lemon juice
1 tsp. Worcestershire sauce
2 bay leaves
1 T. sugar
1 tsp. hot or sweet paprika
Dash of cloves or allspice
4 carrots, cut into chunks as desired
1 rib celery, cut into chunks as desired
2 medium potatoes, peeled and cubed, or 6 new potatoes
8 to 12 oz. fresh mushrooms, sliced
¹/2 cup sherry
¹/2 dry red wine

Season meat with salt and pepper and meat tenderizer if desired, and brown in olive oil with garlic and onions. Add beef bouillon, lemon juice, Worcestershire sauce, bay leaves, sugar, paprika and cloves or allspice. Simmer for 1 to 2 hours, stirring occasionally. Add carrots, celery and potatoes along with sherry and red wine. Cook for 15 minutes. Add mushrooms and cook for 15 minutes longer or until vegetables are tender. Thicken cooking liquid for gravy with a paste of flour and water if desired.

Mary Anne Lecce
Collinsville, IL

BIG GAME

PRAIRIE PRONGHORN ROAST

Pronghorn leg roast, boned
3 T. cooking oil
Dried rosemary
Dried marjoram
Dried thyme
Salt
8 slices bacon
Hot water
1 medium red onion, chopped
$^1/_4$ cup chopped carrot
$^1/_2$ cup chopped leek
$^3/_4$ cup heavy cream
1 cup golden raisins
$^1/_3$ cup gravy flour or cornstarch
4 T. red table wine

Wash and dry roast. Mix oil, rosemary, marjoram, thyme and salt. Brush mixture over roast. Cover and let stand overnight in refrigerator.

Preheat oven to 400°F. Line bottom of roasting pan with 4 slices of bacon. Lightly salt roast and place on top of bacon. Cover roast with remaining bacon slices and place in oven. Once pan juices start to brown, add a little hot water. Baste meat with pan juices and replace evaporated liquid with hot water. After 1 hour of roasting, add onion, carrot and leek. Roast for 1 more hour.

Remove roast from oven, slice into $^1/_2$-inch slices and arrange on warm plate. Add water to juices in pan to make about $^3/_4$ cup liquid; bring to a boil. Add cream and raisins. Use mixture of gravy flour or cornstarch and wine to thicken. Pour gravy over sliced roast and serve.

Michael Witt
Colorado Springs, CO

WILD GAME STROGANOFF

1 1/2 lbs. venison, moose or elk meat (or duck or goose breasts)
1/3 cup flour
Salt and pepper
Nutmeg
1 to 4 T. butter
1 T. chopped garlic
1 cup chopped onion
8 oz. fresh mushrooms, sliced
Juice from fresh lemon half
1 tsp. Worcestershire sauce
1 cup water
1 beef bouillon cube
1/2 cup white wine or sherry
1 cup regular or fat-free sour cream

Slice meat into thin strips on the diagonal. Season flour with salt, pepper and nutmeg and coat meat. Brown meat in butter and garlic in large skillet. Add onion and mushrooms and continue to sauté on low heat until onion and mushrooms are tender, stirring often to prevent sticking. Salt and pepper to taste. Squeeze juice of lemon half over onion and mushrooms while cooking. Add Worcestershire sauce, water, beef bouillon cube and wine. Cover and simmer on low for 45 to 60 minutes. Stir in sour cream and heat through. Serve over noodles.

Mary Anne Lecce
Collinsville, IL

BIG GAME

Antelope Elizabeth

4 1-inch-thick pronghorn steaks
4 T. butter
$^1/_4$ cup chopped red onion
4 T. red table wine
$^1/_2$ cup beef bouillon
$^1/_2$ tsp. sugar
Black pepper, freshly ground
3 T. butter
$^1/_4$ cup brandy
$^1/_4$ cup cream
2 T. whole green peppercorns

Melt 4 tablespoons butter, add onion and cook until onion is golden. Add wine, bouillon and sugar. Continue cooking until liquid is reduced by half. Pepper the steaks, ensuring that both sides are lightly covered. Cook steaks in 3 tablespoons butter to desired doneness. Transfer steaks to warmed plates.

Remove frying pan from heat and allow to cool for 3 minutes. Add brandy and return pan to low heat. Very carefully, light brandy in pan with fireplace match and let flames dance. After alcohol burns off, add cream and peppercorns to original butter and onion mixture. Heat to just below boiling, stirring constantly. Pour sauce over steaks and serve.

Michael Witt
Colorado Springs, CO

SWEET-AND-SOUR ELK

Elk roast
1 pkg. onion soup mix
1/4 cup water
12 oz. apricot preserves
1/2 cup Russian or Catalina salad dressing
1/4 cup brown sugar
1 T. cider vinegar

Combine soup and water and let stand for 15 minutes. Add apricot preserves, salad dressing, brown sugar and vinegar. Salt and pepper meat. Place in greased 9 x 13-inch pan and pour sauce over meat. Cover and bake at 350°F for 45 minutes. Uncover and bake for 30 to 40 minutes longer.

Jerry and Hope Brensinger
Mountain Home, ID

WILD GAME PAPRIKA

2 lbs. moose, elk or venison, cubed
1/2 tsp. meat tenderizer (optional)
1 1/2 T. flour
1/2 tsp. seasoned salt
1/4 tsp. pepper
1/4 tsp. garlic powder
2 T. olive oil
3 cloves garlic, crushed
1 large onion, sliced lengthwise
1 1/2 T. paprika, hot or sweet or both
1/8 tsp. nutmeg
1 T. tomato paste
1 beef bouillon cube
1/2 cup water
1/2 cup port wine
8 oz. fresh mushrooms, quartered

Sprinkle meat with tenderizer if desired. Combine flour, seasoned salt, pepper and garlic powder in a plastic bag. Add cubed meat, close bag and shake to coat meat with flour mixture. Heat olive oil in large skillet and brown meat. Add garlic, onion, paprika, nutmeg, tomato paste, bouillon, water and wine; cover and simmer for 45 minutes. Add mushrooms and simmer, uncovered, for 15 minutes. Serve with noodles.

Mary Anne Lecce
Collinsville, IL

BEAN MEAT CASSEROLE

2 lbs. ground elk, moose, bear or venison
20-oz. can pineapple chunks, drained
16-oz. can pork and beans
16-oz. can kidney beans
1 tsp. dry mustard
1 cup ketchup
¹/₂ cup brown sugar
1 tsp. dill weed
2 tsp. garlic powder

Shape ground meat into walnut-size meatballs and brown until fully cooked in lightly oiled skillet. Add pineapple, pork and beans, kidney beans, dry mustard, ketchup, brown sugar, dill weed and garlic powder, stirring gently. Cover and cook for 10 minutes, stirring occasionally.

Rob Wodzinski
Iron River, MI

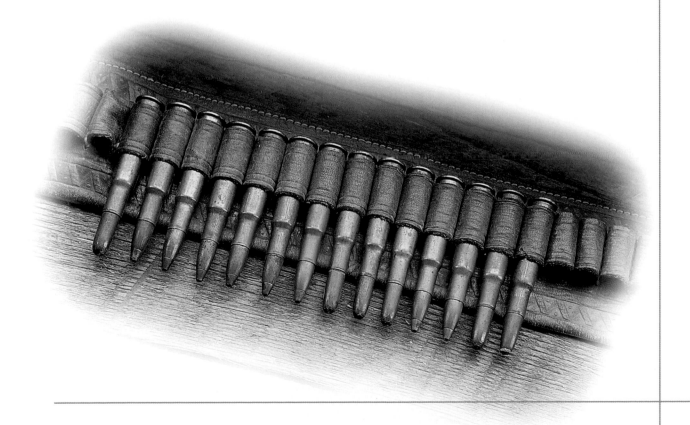

BIG GAME

SMOKED ELK ROAST WITH BRANDY MARINADE

6 to 8 lbs. elk roast
³/4 cup brandy
¹/4 cup olive oil
¹/2 cup Heinz 57
¹/4 cup A-1 Sauce
1³/4 cup red wine
²/3 cup water
1 cup chopped green onion
¹/2 tsp. liquid smoke flavoring
¹/2 T. black pepper
¹/4 tsp. cayenne pepper
5 cloves garlic, finely chopped
Pinch of allspice

Set roast aside and mix remaining ingredients well in a large glass dish. Place roast in marinade and cover. Refrigerate for 2 days, rotating roast often. Remove roast and place on lightly oiled wire rack in smoker. Place remaining marinade in water pan in smoker. Cook slowly until meat thermometer reads 165°F. Slice and serve.

Scott Amick
St. Louis, MO

BIG GAME

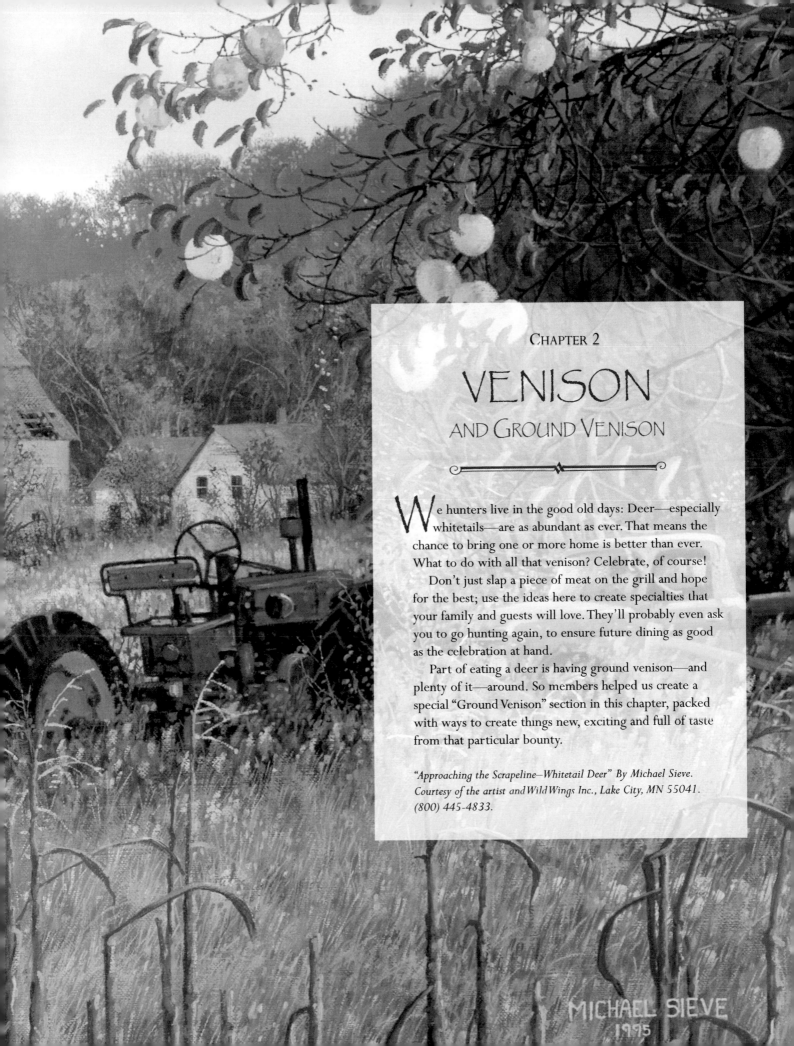

CHAPTER 2

VENISON
AND GROUND VENISON

❦

We hunters live in the good old days: Deer—especially
whitetails—are as abundant as ever. That means the
chance to bring one or more home is better than ever.
What to do with all that venison? Celebrate, of course!

Don't just slap a piece of meat on the grill and hope
for the best; use the ideas here to create specialties that
your family and guests will love. They'll probably even ask
you to go hunting again, to ensure future dining as good
as the celebration at hand.

Part of eating a deer is having ground venison—and
plenty of it—around. So members helped us create a
special "Ground Venison" section in this chapter, packed
with ways to create things new, exciting and full of taste
from that particular bounty.

*"Approaching the Scrapeline–Whitetail Deer" By Michael Sieve.
Courtesy of the artist and Wild Wings Inc., Lake City, MN 55041.
(800) 445-4833.*

MICHAEL SIEVE
1995

VENISON CREOLE

2 lbs. small venison steaks
1/4 cup flour
2 tsp. salt
1/2 tsp. pepper
1/8 tsp. crushed red pepper
2 tsp. paprika
1/2 tsp. garlic powder
2 onions, chopped
1/2 green pepper, chopped
4 T. oil
1/2 cup uncooked rice
2 (16-oz.) cans stewed tomatoes

Pound steaks to tenderize; set aside. Mix flour, salt, pepper, crushed red pepper, paprika and garlic powder. Dredge steaks in flour mixture. Sauté onions and green pepper in oil in cast iron skillet. Remove from pan. Brown steaks and cover with onions and green pepper. Sprinkle with rice. Drain tomatoes, reserving liquid. Add enough water to tomato juice to make 2 cups. Spoon tomatoes over rice and sprinkle with remaining flour mixture. Pour liquid over rice. Cover and bake at 350°F for 1 hour.

Janiece Harshberger
Grayland, WA

BUCK WITH BOURBON

3 lbs. venison, cut into 1/2-inch cubes
2 T. flour
1 tsp. salt
1/4 tsp. freshly ground pepper
1 T. olive oil
2 medium onions, diced
1/2 cup chopped green pepper
2 cloves garlic, minced
1/2 cup beef bouillon
1 cup tomato sauce
1/2 tsp. thyme or crushed rosemary
3 oz. bourbon

Dredge meat in mixture of flour, salt and pepper. Brown meat in olive oil in Dutch oven over medium heat. Remove meat from pan and set aside. Sauté onions, green pepper and garlic in same pan until soft but not brown. Return meat to Dutch oven and add bouillon, tomato sauce, thyme or rosemary and bourbon. Cover and simmer slowly for 2 hours, watching to make sure liquid doesn't dry up.

Duane Musgrave
Grand Rapids, MI

VENISON

VENISON CREOLE

DEERITOS (VENISON BURRITOS)

2¹/₂ to 3 lbs. venison steaks or roast
3 medium onions, 2 cut into chunks and 1 diced
¹/₄ cup butter
Salt and pepper
1 envelope taco seasoning
1 cup water
2 small cans or 1 large can refried beans
16 (8-inch) soft flour tortilla shells
12 oz. shredded cheddar cheese
12 oz. shredded colby and Monterey Jack cheese blend
2 medium jars chunky style salsa
Lettuce, shredded
Tomatoes, diced
Black olives
Sour cream

Remove any tendon and fat from venison. Arrange meat in single layer in shallow baking pan. Cover with onion chunks, dot with butter and season with salt and pepper. Cover with foil and bake at 350°F for 3 to 4 hours. Remove foil and shred meat with fork. Add taco seasoning and 1 cup water, mix well and return to oven for 30 minutes. Warm refried beans and diced onion in saucepan until beans bubble, being careful not to scorch. Lay tortilla shells out and add healthy layer of beans, then meat and a handful of shredded cheddar. Roll deeritos up and place in shallow baking pan. Cover with salsa, top with Colby and Monterey Jack cheese and bake at 325°F for about ¹/₂ hour. Serve with lettuce, tomatoes, olives and sour cream.

Sue Konsdorf
Auburn, MN

VENISON

VENISON CHOW MEIN

1³/4 lbs. venison stew meat

¹/4 cup plus 2 T. soy sauce

1 cup water

1 bunch celery, cut into ¹/2-inch pieces

1 onion, chopped

2 T. cornstarch

¹/4 cup water

Small can sliced water chestnuts

20-oz. can bean sprouts, drained

Small can mushrooms

Salt and pepper

Remove all tallow from venison and dice meat. Brown in large skillet. Add soy sauce and 1 cup water and simmer for 2 minutes. Add celery, including leaves, and onion. Simmer for 1¹/2 hours. Blend cornstarch with ¹/4 cup water and stir into meat mixture. Add water chestnuts, bean sprouts and mushrooms. Season with salt and pepper to taste and heat through. Serve over rice with chow mein noodles.

Floyd E. Peters Sr.
Superior, WI

VENISON JERKY

2¹/2 lbs. venison, cut into strips

2 T. Worcestershire sauce

¹/4 cup soy sauce

2 T. garlic salt

2 T. black pepper

2 T. liquid smoke flavoring

¹/2 cup brown sugar

Mix all ingredients except meat in large bowl or container. Cover and refrigerate for 1 to 2 days, mixing well each day. Place toothpick through each strip and hang on top oven rack. Bake at 175°F for 6 to 8 hours.

Raymond Bond
Portland, MI

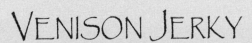

VENISON

Prosciutto and Mozzarella-Stuffed Venison Loin
with Sun-Dried Tomato and White Wine Sauce

¹/2 venison loin (backstrap)
Fresh pepper
Prosciutto (about 6 slices)
Mozzarella cheese slices (about 8 slices)
Egg
Milk
Flour
¹/2 cup white wine
1 shallot, finely chopped
6 to 8 sun-dried tomatoes, chopped
2 cups heavy cream
4 to 6 T. cold butter
Lemon juice
Salt and pepper

Open loin with knife, like a jelly roll, and lay flat. Season with pepper. Place 1 slice prosciutto and 1 slice mozzarella cheese on loin, roll up and tie with string as needed. Make wash of egg and milk. Dip loin in egg wash and then in flour seasoned with salt and pepper. Repeat. Sear on all sides in ¹/4-inch of hot oil. Transfer to baking dish and bake at 375° to 400°F for 30 minutes. In medium saucepan, combine white wine, shallot and sun-dried tomatoes. Boil until liquid is reduced by ³/4, add cream. Stir and cook to desired thickness. Whisk in cold butter, lemon juice and salt and pepper to taste. Carve loin into ³/4-inch slices, cover with sauce and serve hot.

Ken Minnich
Neptune, NJ

VENISON

TWICE-COOKED VENISON

3 to 4 lbs. venison rump roast chops
$^1/_4$ cup vegetable oil
$^1/_2$ cup Worcestershire sauce
$^1/_2$ tsp. garlic powder
$^1/_2$ tsp. seasoned salt
Butter
1 large onion, chopped
1 bottle chili sauce
$^1/_4$ cup barbecue sauce
Salt and pepper

Slice venison into $^1/_2$-inch slices. For marinade, mix oil, garlic powder, Worcestershire sauce and seasoned salt. Marinate sliced venison in refrigerator for at least 2 hours. Brown meat and onion in butter. Place in roaster or slow cooker and add chili sauce, barbecue sauce and season with salt and pepper to taste. Bake at 325°F for about 2 hours or until tender or slow cook for at least 8 hours on low.

L.C. Forslund
Warren, MN

BRANDIED VENISON

1 venison tenderloin
Flour
Garlic salt
Pepper
4 T. melted butter or margarine
1 cup water
$^1/_2$ lb. mushrooms, sliced
2 T. brandy
$^1/_2$ cup sour cream

Mix flour with garlic salt and pepper. Slice tenderloin in $^1/_2$-inch pieces and coat well with seasoned flour. Pound coated venison thoroughly with mallet and brown in butter. Transfer meat to paper towel-lined plate to drain. Mix some flour or cornstarch with water; add to pan drippings, stirring well to dissolve browned bits. When gravy is thickened, return venison to skillet and add mushrooms and brandy. Cook until mushrooms are hot. Add sour cream and heat through. Serve over hot biscuits, rice, mashed potatoes or pasta.

Robert Bornemann
Waterford, CA

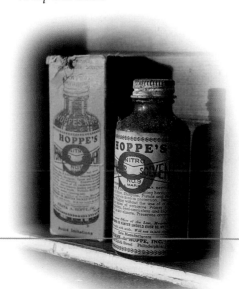

VENISON

MA'S KITCHEN JERKY

Venison strips, cut $^1/_4$-inch thick
$^1/_4$ cup soy sauce
$^1/_4$ cup Worcestershire sauce
$^1/_4$ cup brown sugar
2 T. maple syrup
1 T. honey
1 T. minced garlic
$^3/_4$ tsp. cayenne pepper
$^1/_2$ tsp. black pepper
$^1/_4$ tsp. ground cloves
1 tsp. liquid smoke flavoring

Mix all ingredients except meat. Add venison strips to marinade and refrigerate overnight. Dehydrate using oven or dehydrator.

Eric Lucido
Londonderry, NH

VENISON SWISS PEPPER STEAK

$1^1/_2$ lbs. venison, cut into $^1/_2$-inch pieces
1 medium onion, diced
1 green pepper, diced
2 cloves garlic, minced
$^1/_2$ cup flour
$^1/_2$ tsp. salt
$^1/_4$ tsp. pepper
$^1/_4$ tsp. oregano
12-oz. can tomato sauce or spaghetti sauce

Sauté onion, green pepper and garlic in butter until soft but not brown. Mix flour, salt, pepper and oregano in paper or plastic bag. Add venison and shake to coat meat. Remove and brown in oil. Layer meat and vegetables in casserole or oven bag. Cover with tomato or spaghetti sauce and bake at 350°F for $1^1/_2$ hours. Serve over spaghetti or rice.

Variation: Omit green pepper. Substitute tomato sauce or spaghetti sauce with cream of mushroom soup mixed with $^1/_2$ cup milk. Bake as instructed above and serve over hot buttered noodles.

Robert Gross
Vincentown, NJ

VENISON

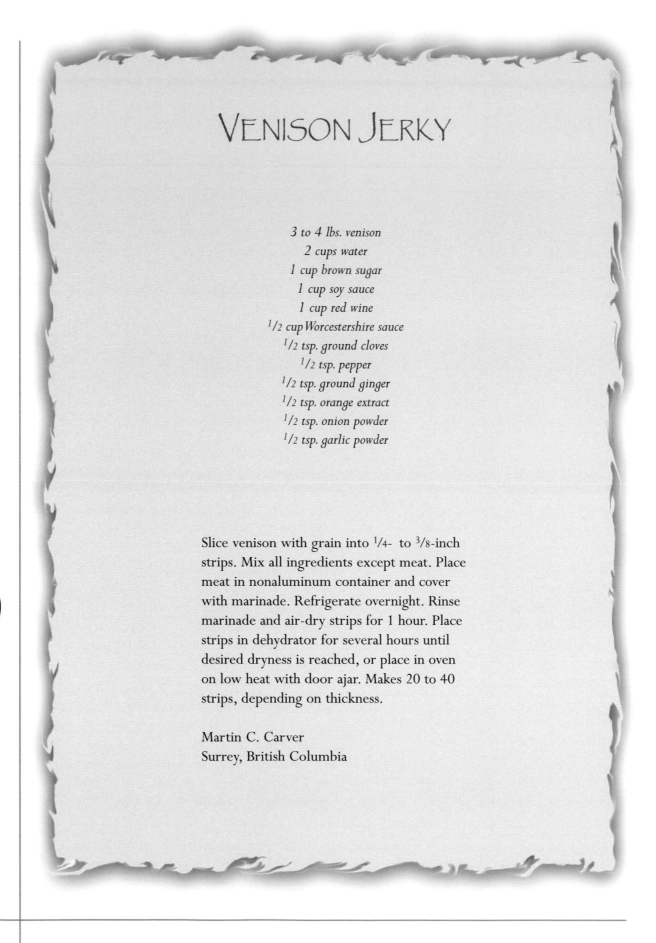

VENISON JERKY

3 to 4 lbs. venison
2 cups water
1 cup brown sugar
1 cup soy sauce
1 cup red wine
$^1/_2$ cup Worcestershire sauce
$^1/_2$ tsp. ground cloves
$^1/_2$ tsp. pepper
$^1/_2$ tsp. ground ginger
$^1/_2$ tsp. orange extract
$^1/_2$ tsp. onion powder
$^1/_2$ tsp. garlic powder

Slice venison with grain into $^1/_4$- to $^3/_8$-inch strips. Mix all ingredients except meat. Place meat in nonaluminum container and cover with marinade. Refrigerate overnight. Rinse marinade and air-dry strips for 1 hour. Place strips in dehydrator for several hours until desired dryness is reached, or place in oven on low heat with door ajar. Makes 20 to 40 strips, depending on thickness.

Martin C. Carver
Surrey, British Columbia

Venison Hoagies

1 large venison backstrap, cut into $^1/_2$-inch cubes
1 medium green pepper, sliced
1 medium yellow or red pepper, sliced
1 medium onion, sliced
4 oz. fresh mushrooms, sliced
4 hoagie rolls
4 oz. mozzarella cheese, grated

Fry cubed venison in oil until cooked. Sauté peppers, onion and mushrooms in butter until tender. Cut pocket in rolls, being careful not to cut roll in half. Place venison cubes on bottom of pocket and layer vegetables on top. Top with mozzarella cheese. Microwave hoagies for about 30 seconds or until cheese is melted.

David Huffman
Charlotte, NC

Hunters' Stew

2 lbs. venison, cubed
4 cups water or beef broth
6-oz. can tomato paste
6 carrots, cut into chunks
2 onions, cut into chunks
2 cups chopped celery
Oregano
Garlic powder
Salt and pepper

In large, heavy kettle brown venison in oil until caramelized. Add broth and tomato paste. Simmer for 2 hours. Add carrots, onions, celery, oregano, garlic powder, salt and pepper; cook for about 30 minutes or until vegetables are tender. Thicken with flour and water to desired consistency. Serve over baking powder biscuits, mashed potatoes or noodles.

Ray J. Lear III
Watertown, NY

VENISON

VENISON STIR-FRY
WITH BROCCOLI AND APPLES

$1^1/2$ lbs. venison, cut into 2 x $^1/2$-inch strips
3 T. sugar
$^1/4$ cup soy sauce
1 tsp. crushed mint or dill
2 T. olive oil
1 T. butter
1 bunch broccoli florets
3 broccoli stalks, peeled and sliced to $^1/2$ inch (optional)
1 medium onion, cut into wedges
1 small or $^1/2$ large apple, cut into $^1/2$-inch chunks

Mix sugar, soy sauce and mint or dill in medium bowl. Coat venison with sauce mixture and set aside. Heat oil and butter in wok or large skillet on medium high. Add venison and sauce and cook for about 4 minutes. Remove venison from sauce and set aside. Add broccoli and onion to sauce. Cover and cook until tender. Add venison and apple to wok and mix together. Serve over rice.

Dale Pinto
Crafton, PA

VENISON

VENISON CHILI

4 lbs. venison, cut into $^1/_2$-inch cubes or ground
2 medium onions, chopped
1 green pepper, chopped
2 cloves garlic, minced
1 tsp. chopped jalapeño pepper
6 T. oil
8 T. chili powder
1 T. ground cumin
2 tsp. garlic salt
1 tsp. oregano
$^1/_4$ tsp. Tabasco sauce
2 cans beer, divided
28-oz. can whole tomatoes
12-oz. can tomato sauce
6-oz. can tomato paste
4-oz. can diced green chiles
2 bay leaves

Sauté onions, green pepper, garlic and jalapeño in 2 T. oil until onions are transparent; set aside. Brown venison in 4 T. oil and combine with vegetables in large pot. Mix chili powder, cumin, garlic salt, oregano, Tabasco sauce and 1 can of beer; let sauce mixture stand a few minutes. Add sauce mixture, whole tomatoes, tomato sauce and tomato paste, chiles, bay leaves and second can of beer to vegetables and venison in pot; stir. Cover and simmer for 3 hours, stirring often.

Robert Gross
Vincentown, NJ

Venison and Scalloped Potatoes

Venison or elk roast
1¹/₂ cups milk
1 tsp. garlic powder
³/₄ cup flour
Potatoes
2 cups chopped onion
Salt and pepper
3¹/₂ cups grated cheddar cheese

Slice roast into $^1/_4$-inch-thick pieces and set aside. Mix 2 cups water with milk and garlic powder in a saucepan; bring to a boil. Whisk flour into 1 cup water and stir into milk sauce to thicken. Slice enough potatoes $^1/_8$-inch thick to fill 10 x 15 baking dish half full. Sprinkle with onions, salt and pepper. Pour sauce over potatoes and cover with meat slices. Top with cheese. Bake at 350°F for 1 to 1$^1/_2$ hours or until potatoes are tender.

Lance Goucher
Phoenix, OR

Oriental Venison Sticks

Venison strips, 1¹/₂-inch wide x ¹/₄-inch thick
¹/₄ cup soy sauce
¹/₃ cup teriyaki sauce
¹/₃ cup honey
2 T. oil
1 T. chopped garlic
1 tsp. ground ginger

For marinade, mix soy sauce, teriyaki sauce, honey, oil, garlic and ginger. Pour over venison strips and refrigerate for several hours, turning often. Soak bamboo skewers in water for 10 minutes. Thread venison strips onto skewers to lay flat. Grill over very hot coals for 2 to 4 minutes on each side. Serve immediately.

Kevin Tramutola
Staten Island, NY

VENISON

VENISON STROGANOFF

2 lbs. venison, cubed
Salt and pepper
2 large onions, sliced
2 beef bouillon cubes
2 qts. water
1 cup cooking sherry or wine
Flour
Water
1 cup sour cream

Brown venison in oil in heavy kettle. Add onions, salt, pepper, bouillon cubes and water. Bring to a boil, reduce heat and simmer for several hours. Add cooking sherry and thicken with mixture of flour and water. Remove from heat and add sour cream. Serve over noodles.

Ray J. Lear III
Watertown, NY

POPPY'S JERKY

2 to 3 lbs. venison or moose, cut into strips
$^1/_2$ cup brown sugar
$^1/_2$ cup hickory liquid smoke flavoring
1 cup soy sauce

Mix sugar, smoke flavoring and soy sauce and let stand for 5 minutes. Add meat and marinate overnight or for at least 3 hours in airtight container in refrigerator. Drain and place on dehydrator trays. Do not overlap strips. Cook for 8 to 9 hours. If drying in oven, place on top rack over pan to catch drips. Bake at 150°F or lowest setting for 6 to 8 hours or until meat is dried.

John W. Larabie
Griffith, Ontario

Venison Oriental

1 lb. venison flank steak or other tender portion
1 lb. medium to large shrimp (optional)
1 lb. medium scallops (optional)
1 cup vegetable oil
1 green pepper, cut into 1-inch pieces
1 red pepper, cut into 1-inch pieces
1 onion, cut into 1-inch pieces
2 tomatoes, cut into 1-inch pieces
1 can sliced bamboo shoots, drained
1 can water chestnuts, drained
1 can baby corn, drained

Marinade

$^1/_2$ cup chicken broth

$^1/_4$ cup water

1 tsp. cornstarch

1 T. soy sauce

1 tsp. sesame oil (or vegetable oil)

$^3/_4$ cup sugar

$2^1/_2$ T. ketchup

Seasoning Sauce

2 tsp. rice wine or dry sherry

$^3/_4$ tsp. sugar

$3^1/_4$ T. soy sauce

$1^3/_4$ tsp. minced fresh ginger root
   (or ground ginger)

$^1/_2$ tsp. black pepper

$1^3/_4$ tsp. cornstarch

4 T. vegetable oil

Prepare marinade and set aside. Slice venison into thin strips at an angle across grain and cut strips into 2-inch pieces. Add venison strips to marinade; mix well. Refrigerate for at least 1 or 2 hours. Prepare seasoning sauce, mix well and set aside. Heat oil in wok or large skillet over medium heat for 1 minute. Stir-fry marinated venison until lightly browned. Remove venison with slotted spoon, draining well over wok. Repeat with shrimp and scallops if desired. Remove all but a little more than $^1/_4$ cup oil from wok. Heat remaining oil over high heat for 30 seconds. Stir-fry green pepper 2 to 3 minutes; remove with slotted spoon, draining well over wok. If necessary, add no more than 1 tablespoon oil. Repeat with red pepper, onion, tomatoes, each in turn. Stir-fry water chestnuts, bamboo shoots and baby corn for 2 to 3 minutes and add peppers, onion and tomatoes, stir-frying for another 1 to 2 minutes. Stir seasoning sauce and add to wok; stir-fry for 2 to 3 minutes. Add venison (and seafood if you wish), mix well, heat through and serve over rice.

Robert Stender
Brooklyn, NY

VENISON

Venison Pizzaiola with Polenta

2 lbs. venison steaks, cut crosswise into thin strips
1/2 cup olive oil
1/4 cup butter
1/2 lb. wild or commercial mushrooms
1 medium onion, thinly sliced
3 cloves garlic, thinly sliced
8-oz. can plum tomatoes
1/2 cup chopped parsley
1 tsp. oregano
1 cup red wine
1 cup freshly grated Parmesan cheese

Polenta

4 cups water
1 cup cornmeal
1 tsp. salt
5 T. butter
1/4 cup freshly grated Parmesan cheese
2 cups diced mozzarella cheese

Heat oil and butter in large skillet over medium-high heat and brown meat on all sides. Lift meat with slotted spoon and place on platter. Sauté mushrooms until lightly browned and transfer to platter. Sauté onion and garlic until lightly browned. Add tomatoes and mash lightly with fork. Bring to a boil and stir in parsley, oregano, wine, Parmesan cheese, venison and mushrooms. Cover and simmer 1 1/2 hours, stirring occasionally. About 1/2 hour before serving, prepare polenta.

To prepare polenta: Bring 3 cups of water to a boil. Stir cornmeal into 1 cup of cold water and pour mixture into boiling water, stirring constantly. Add salt and cook on medium heat, stirring constantly, for 10 to 15 minutes or until mixture is very thick. Remove from heat and stir in butter and cheeses. Mound polenta on platter, make an impression in center and spoon in venison and sauce.

Andi Flanagan
Seward, AK

Venison Fried Rice

2 cups chopped, cooked venison
Oil
Soy sauce
3/4 cup chopped onion
1 cup cooked peas
1 cup scrambled eggs
4 cups cooked rice, cooled

Prepare rice and set aside. Heat wok or large skillet until hot. Add oil and soy sauce. Sauté onion lightly. Add venison, peas and eggs and toss lightly. Add cooked, cooled rice and stir until mixture is hot, adding soy sauce to taste if desired.

Ray J. Lear III
Watertown, NY

Baked Steak

1 1/2 to 2 lbs. venison or elk round steak
Garlic butter
28-oz. can tomato sauce
1/4 cup red wine
1/2 tsp. ground cumin
1 clove garlic, diced
1 large onion, sliced
2 to 3 sweet bell peppers, sliced
Salt and pepper

Cut steaks into serving pieces and pound with meat mallet or rub with tenderizer. Melt enough garlic butter in skillet to cover bottom. Brown meat in hot skillet, adding more butter if necessary. Place tomato sauce, wine, cumin, garlic, onion and peppers in roasting pan and add meat. Salt and pepper to taste. Make sure meat is covered with sauce; add more if necessary. Cover and bake at 325°F for 45 to 60 minutes or until meat is fork tender, stirring once during baking. Serve over mashed potatoes.

Dave Kulaszewski Sr.
Cleveland, OH

VENISON

Venison Fajitas

2 lbs. venison or other big game meat, sliced into $^1/_4$-inch strips
6 oz. lime juice
2 T. olive oil
3 cloves garlic, crushed
1 tsp. cumin
$1^1/_2$ tsp. paprika
$1^1/_2$ tsp. oregano
$1^1/_2$ tsp. cayenne pepper
$^1/_4$ cup dehydrated onion flakes
1 tsp. seasoned salt
$^1/_4$ to $^1/_2$ tsp. crushed red pepper flakes (optional)
$^1/_2$ cup dry white wine or sherry
1 T. olive oil
2 onions, sliced
1 red pepper, cut up
1 green pepper, cut up
6-inch flour tortillas
Sour cream
Salsa
Guacamole

Puncture meat liberally with fork. In a glass container, mix lime juice, olive oil, garlic, cumin, paprika, oregano, cayenne pepper, onion flakes, seasoned salt, crushed red pepper flakes and wine. Add meat to marinade and refrigerate for 5 to 6 hours or overnight. Remove meat from marinade and set aside. Transfer marinade to saucepan and heat to boiling. Grill meat quickly over hot barbecue flame, basting with marinade. Sauté onions and peppers in olive oil in skillet for about 10 minutes, until vegetables are cooked but not brown. Wrap cooked meat and vegetables in tortillas and top with sour cream, salsa and guacamole.

Mary Anne Lecce
Collinsville, IL

VENISON

Venison Stewed in Cranberry Chutney

2 lbs. venison stew meat, cut into chunks
3 T. oil
1 large onion, chopped
2 ribs celery, chopped
2 cloves garlic, minced
2 cups boiling water
2^1/$_2$ cups cranberries
^{3}/$_4$ cup raisins
2 T. balsamic vinegar or cider vinegar
2 T. brown sugar
^{1}/$_4$ tsp. cinnamon
^{1}/$_4$ tsp. ground ginger
^{1}/$_4$ tsp. ground cloves
^{1}/$_4$ tsp. cayenne pepper
Grated zest and juice of ^{1}/$_2$ lemon

Heat oil in Dutch oven and brown meat on all sides. Remove meat and sauté onion, celery and garlic until just golden. Add meat, boiling water, cranberries, raisins, vinegar, brown sugar, cinnamon, ginger, cloves, cayenne pepper, lemon zest and lemon juice. Cover and simmer 1^1/$_2$ hours or until venison is fork tender. Serve with fluffy white rice and stewed pears.

Andi Flanagan
Seward, AK

MEXICAN CARNE SECA (JERKY)

3 lbs. venison, sliced across grain into
   2- x $^1/_8$-inch strips
1 large yellow onion, sliced
2 cloves garlic, sliced
2 tsp. oregano
1 tsp. chili powder
$^1/_4$ tsp. cumin seed
$^1/_2$ tsp. fresh cracked peppercorns
$^3/_4$ cup red wine vinegar

Mix all ingredients in large glass bowl or plastic freezer bag and chill for 24 hours. Arrange on racks and dry in oven at 200°F for 6 to 7 hours, alternating pans and racks every 1$^1/_2$ hours. Good in Corn and Jerky Chowder (see page 71).

Andi Flanagan
Seward, AK

EASY VEGETABLE SOUP

1 lb. boneless venison round steak
1 can diced tomatoes
3 cups water
2 potatoes, peeled and cubed
2 onions, diced
3 ribs celery, sliced
2 carrots, sliced
3 beef bouillon cubes
$^1/_2$ tsp. dried basil
$^1/_2$ tsp. dried oregano
$^1/_2$ tsp. salt
$^1/_4$ tsp. pepper
1$^1/_2$ cups frozen mixed vegetables

Combine round steak, tomatoes, water, potatoes, onions, celery, carrots, bouillon, basil, oregano, salt and pepper in slow cooker. Cover and cook on high for 6 hours. Add frozen mixed vegetables; cover and cook on high for 2 hours longer or until meat and vegetables are tender.

Richard Baker
Lima, OH

Venison Tenderloin Marsala

1 to 2 lbs. venison tenderloin, trimmed
Nonstick cooking spray
1 T. minced garlic
$1/2$ cup dry Marsala or $1/4$ cup dry red wine
$1/4$ cup chicken broth
1 T. tomato paste
5 cups sliced fresh mushrooms
1 T. snipped fresh parsley

Cut tenderloin diagonally into $1/4$-inch thick slices. Spray skillet with nonstick spray and cook venison slices on both sides over medium heat until tender. Remove and keep warm. Sauté garlic in skillet for 1 minute over medium heat. Combine Marsala or red wine, broth and tomato paste in small bowl. Add sauce and mushrooms to skillet and bring to a boil. Reduce heat and cook uncovered for about 10 minutes or until liquid is reduced by half. Return venison to skillet and heat through.

Transfer meat and sauce to a warm platter and sprinkle with parsley. Serve with wild rice or noodles. Garnish with additional parsley if desired.

Patrick Gorczyca
Jackson, MI

Tasty Chops

4 to 8 venison or elk chops (1 to $1^1/2$ per person)
Small jar dill pickles, chopped
1 large onion, chopped
4 cloves garlic, minced
$1/4$ to $1/3$ lb. bacon, chopped
Seasoned salt
1 potato, sliced, per person
1 carrot, sliced, per person

Chop pickles; reserve pickle juice. Brown chops in skillet with oil. Sprinkle lightly with seasoned salt, chopped pickles, onion, garlic and bacon. Pour pickle juice over meat. Braise in skillet for $2^1/2$ to 3 hours until meat is tender, turning meat every 30 minutes and adding water as necessary to keep liquid at $1/2$ inch. Add sliced potato and carrot during last 30 to 45 minutes.

Linda Kuker
Valparaiso, IN

Easy Venison Stir-Fry

Venison tenderloin, cut into thin strips
1 tsp. ground ginger or fresh ginger root
2 T. red wine
1 tsp. garlic powder
1 tsp. sugar
2 tsp. soy sauce
2 T. peanut oil
2 cups broccoli florets
1 cup sliced or chopped onion
2 tsp. cornstarch

Mix ginger, wine, garlic powder, sugar and soy sauce. Add venison strips to this marinade and refrigerate for several hours. Heat oil in wok or large skillet and stir-fry broccoli and onion. Remove vegetables. Stir-fry drained venison until red color disappears. Stir cornstarch into marinade; pour marinade into skillet. Return vegetables to skillet; cook until sauce bubbles and has thickened slightly. Serve over rice.

Gavin Bennett
Muskogee, OK

Venison with Roquefort Butter

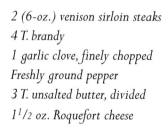

2 (6-oz.) venison sirloin steaks
4 T. brandy
1 garlic clove, finely chopped
Freshly ground pepper
3 T. unsalted butter, divided
1$^1/_2$ oz. Roquefort cheese

Mix brandy, garlic and pepper in covered glass dish and marinate steaks in refrigerator for 4 hours. Mix 2 tablespoons butter with cheese, form into a roll, wrap and refrigerate. Melt 1 tablespoon butter in heavy skillet. Drain meat, reserving marinade. Fry meat for about 3 minutes per side, turning once. Transfer steaks to warm plate and add marinade to skillet. Bring to a boil, scraping bottom of pan to loosen browned bits. Pour marinade over meat and top each steak with 2 slices of cheese/butter roll.

Jim Matousek
Herkimer, NY

MARINATED VENISON ROAST

5-lb. venison roast
8 ginger snaps (optional)
2 cups water
1 T. water
1 T. salt
$^1/_2$ tsp. pepper
$^1/_2$ tsp. ground cloves
3 onions, chopped
1$^1/_2$ cups chopped celery
2 cups vinegar
$^1/_4$ cup brown sugar
1 bay leaf
3 carrots, diced
2 T. bacon drippings or vegetable oil

Set roast and ginger snaps aside. Combine remaining ingredients to make marinade. Marinate roast for 1 to 2 days in refrigerator. Bake roast in marinade at 325°F for 3 hours. Cool and skim grease off top. If desired, add ginger snaps to gravy to enhance flavor.

Les Zearing
Bagley, MN

TY'S VENISON JERKY

5 lbs. venison, duck or goose, sliced into strips
$^1/_2$ cup Morton's Tender Quick or meat
    tenderizer
$^1/_2$ cup brown sugar
2 bay leaves
2 cloves garlic, minced
1 quart water
3 T. liquid smoke flavoring

Mix all ingredients except meat. Add meat and marinate for 20 hours. Place marinated meat on broiling pan and bake at 200°F for 3 to 4 hours.

Aaron Franklund
Bismarck, ND

Venison Parmigiana

4 venison chops or venison steaks
1 egg, beaten
1 tsp. salt
$^1/_8$ tsp. pepper
$^1/_2$ cup fine, dry bread crumbs
$^1/_4$ cup grated Parmesan cheese
3 T. butter

Tomato Sauce

2 T. butter or margarine
$^2/_3$ cup chopped onion
$^1/_4$ cup finely chopped green pepper
8-oz. can tomato sauce
$^1/_4$ tsp. basil
Salt and pepper
$1^1/_2$ cups shredded mozzarella cheese

Combine salt and pepper with egg, and add bread crumbs and Parmesan cheese. Dip chops or steaks in egg and coat with crumb mixture. Brown venison in butter in large skillet over medium heat. Reduce heat to low and cook for 30 minutes or until meat is tender. Prepare sauce; cook onion and green pepper in a saucepan for about 5 minutes in butter. Add tomato sauce and basil. Season to taste with salt and pepper; simmer uncovered for 10 minutes. When venison is done, arrange in a baking dish. Pour sauce over meat and top with mozzarella cheese. Place under broiler until cheese is melted and lightly browned.

Rick Fusinatto
Peru, IL

VENISON

Slow-Cooked Italian Venison

5 lb. venison roast
3 cans French onion soup
1¹/₂ T. minced garlic
1 T. Italian seasoning
1 tsp. basil flakes
2 tsp. salt
1 tsp. onion powder
Mozzarella cheese (sliced or shredded)

Pour French onion soup over meat in slow cooker. Add enough water to cover meat and add garlic, Italian seasoning, basil, salt and onion powder. Cook on high for 6 to 8 hours. When roast is done, remove from cooker and shred meat. Mix shredded meat back into juice. Serve on hoagie bun topped with melted mozzarella cheese and with pepperoncinis on the side.

Jeff Moon
Wyanet, IL

Marinated Venison Steaks

4 venison steaks
¹/₂ cup olive oil
1 clove garlic, minced
¹/₄ cup dry white wine
2 T. soy sauce
1 tsp. dry mustard
Juice of ¹/₂ lemon
Salt and pepper

Combine olive oil, garlic, wine, soy sauce, dry mustard, lemon juice, salt and pepper. Place steaks in shallow pan and cover with marinade. Refrigerate for at least 4 hours or overnight. Remove steaks from marinade, reserving liquid. Grill over hot fire or broil indoors for 2 to 3 minutes per side, brushing frequently with reserved marinade. Do not overcook.

John R. McAfoose
Sandy Lake, PA

No-Salt Jerky

4 lbs. venison

³/4 cup cider vinegar

³/4 cup brown sugar

3 cups apple cider

¹/4 cup diced onion

1 T. garlic powder

Tabasco or other hot sauce (optional)

Place meat in freezer until firm but not frozen, about 4 to 5 hours. Use sharp knife to slice into strips ³/4- to ³/16-inch thick. Mix vinegar, brown sugar, cider, onion, garlic powder and Tabasco sauce; pour marinade over meat strips in nonaluminum bowl. Add water to cover if necessary. Refrigerate for 12 hours or longer. Arrange meat on cookie sheets and dry at 150° to 160°F for 5 to 6 hours, flipping strips once. So that meat dries but doesn't cook, prop oven door open ¹/2 inch to let moisture escape.

Robert Gross
Vincentown, NJ

VENISON

Herbed Venison Pilaf

1 cup cooked venison, diced

¹/4 cup butter

2 cups uncooked long-grain rice

1 cup finely chopped celery

¹/2 cup finely chopped onion

4 cups beef broth

1 tsp. Worcestershire sauce

1 tsp. soy sauce

1 tsp. dried oregano

1 tsp. dried thyme

1 tsp. dried parsley

1 tsp. salt-free seasoning blend

Sauté rice, celery and onion in butter until tender. Add venison. Pour rice mixture into greased 2-quart casserole. Combine beef broth, Worcestershire sauce, soy sauce, oregano, thyme, parsley and seasoning blend. Pour sauce mixture over rice. Cover and bake at 325°F for about 50 minutes or until rice is done.

Joseph Allen
Chester, VT

GRILLED STUFFED VENISON CHOPS
WITH ROQUEFORT WHISKEY SAUCE

2 extra-thick venison or lamb chops
1 tsp. butter or margarine
1 bunch leeks, washed twice and drained then sliced
$^1/_2$ lb. chanterelle, morel or button mushrooms, sliced
2 oz. Roquefort (blue) cheese, crumbled
1 tsp. flour
Salt and pepper
$^1/_2$ tsp. garlic powder
1 oz. whiskey
4 oz. brown gravy, made ahead

Season chops with salt, pepper and garlic powder. Cut a pocket between ribs and set chops aside. Sauté mushrooms and leeks in butter until leeks are translucent, about 5 minutes on medium low. Salt and pepper to taste. Add flour to thicken. Set aside to cool, saving pan flavorings. Stuff chops through slit and remove any leftover mushroom mixture. Stuff half of blue cheese into chops, reserving half for sauce. Brown chops evenly on grill, about 10 minutes. Roast in oven at 350°F for 45 minutes for medium rare, 50 minutes for medium. While chops are roasting, prepare brown gravy and set aside. Add whiskey, more or less to taste, to drippings in skillet. Cook on medium heat, being careful not to flame, until liquid is nearly evaporated. Add brown gravy and simmer for 2 minutes. Add remaining blue cheese and cook 1 minute more. Set aside. When chops are ready, top with sauce and serve with braised red cabbage and apples (below).

Kevin White
McKinleyville, CA

BRAISED RED CABBAGE AND APPLES

1 head red cabbage, cored and shredded
1 cup red wine or balsamic vinegar
$^1/_4$ cup sugar, brown or white
3 tart apples, peeled, cored and sliced
1 to 2 T. caraway seed or fennel seed
1 tsp. black pepper

Kevin White
McKinleyville, CA

Combine all ingredients in large pot and bring to a boil on medium heat. Reduce heat, stirring often for about 20 minutes. Salt and pepper to taste. *Or, combine all ingredients in Dutch oven, cover with lid and bake for 1 hour and 15 minutes at 350°F. Remove from oven and stir.*

Allow cabbage to cool. Serve hot as a side dish or cold as a salad.

VENISON

TENDER VENISON STEAK

Venison or elk steaks
Meat tenderizer
1/2 tsp. salt
1/2 tsp. pepper
1 T. basil
1 T. oregano
1 cup flour
3 T. vegetable oil
1/2 cup chopped onions
1/2 cup chopped mushrooms
Cornstarch
1/2 cup milk

Make 1/8-inch cuts with sharp knife on both sides of steak. Lightly coat steaks with meat tenderizer and refrigerate for at least 12 hours. Mix salt, pepper, basil and oregano with flour; coat steaks in mixture. Brown steaks in hot oil. Add enough water to cover steaks. Turn heat to medium low, cover and simmer for 50 minutes, adding more water as needed. Add onions and mushrooms and simmer for another 10 minutes. Remove steaks from skillet. Shake milk and cornstarch and add to pan juices. Simmer to consistency of gravy. Return steaks to skillet and serve with mashed potatoes, corn and a big glass of milk.

Aaron Pritchard
Palm Bay, FL

VENISON

KATHY'S VENISON TERIYAKI

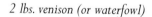

2 lbs. venison (or waterfowl)
1/2 cup soy sauce
2 T. brown sugar
2 tsp. ground ginger
1 T. minced garlic
2 T. olive oil
1 T. chopped chives
1/8 tsp. ground cloves

Mix all ingredients except meat and place in plastic bag or glass baking dish with meat. Refrigerate in marinade at least one day, turning meat several times. Remove meat from marinade and set aside. Heat marinade in saucepan to boiling. Cook meat on grill to desired doneness, basting with excess marinade.

Dennis L. Morgan
Livonia, NY

VENISON BACON PARMESAN

2 venison steaks, $^1/4$-inch thick
$^1/2$ cup Parmesan salad dressing
1 tsp. fresh horseradish
$^1/2$ tsp. garlic powder
4 tsp. grated Parmesan cheese
Seasoned salt
Freshly ground black pepper
2 strips bacon

Mix salad dressing, horseradish, garlic powder, Parmesan cheese, seasoned salt and pepper; set aside. Fry bacon in large skillet until crisp. Remove bacon and set aside. Brown steaks. Add half of dressing mixture to top of steaks. Flip steaks and add remaining half to other side. Cook steaks for 2 minutes more on each side. Transfer steaks to warm plate. Stir pan juices until they thicken into sauce. Pour sauce over steaks and serve.

Edward J. Fleming
Scrgcantsville, NJ

CORN AND JERKY CHOWDER

2 cups Mexican Carne Seca or other jerky,
  broken into small pieces and loosely packed
  (see recipe on page 60)
$^1/4$ lb. salt pork, diced
2 medium onions, chopped
2 medium potatoes, diced
$^1/4$ cup chopped green pepper
1 cup boiling water
2 cups cream-style corn
$3^1/2$ cups milk
Pinch of basil
Pinch of paprika
Salt and freshly ground pepper

Brown salt pork in skillet and transfer to soup pot. Sauté onions, potatoes and green pepper for about 10 minutes and add to soup pot. Put jerky in skillet, pour boiling water over and simmer for 5 minutes. Add jerky, corn, milk, basil and paprika to soup pot and simmer over low heat for 30 minutes. Salt and pepper to taste.

Andi Flanagan
Seward, AK

VENISON

Venison Kabobs

1 to 2 lbs. venison, cut into 1$\frac{1}{2}$- to 2-inch cubes
1 large onion, cut into large pieces
1 green pepper, cut into large pieces
1 red pepper, cut into large pieces
Cherry tomatoes
Mushrooms (optional)

MARINADE

$\frac{1}{4}$ cup oil
$\frac{1}{4}$ cup soy sauce
$\frac{1}{4}$ cup lemon juice
2 T. Worcestershire sauce
1 clove garlic, minced
1 tsp. black pepper
1 tsp. dry or prepared mustard

Mix marinade ingredients together. Pour marinade over meat and refrigerate for 8 to 24 hours. Shake or stir occasionally (at least every 4 hours). Place venison cubes on skewer, alternating with vegetables. Grill to desired doneness.

David W. Foxworth
APO AE

VENISON

EASY VENISON BURRITOS

1 lb. leftover venison roast, shredded
4-oz. can diced green chili peppers
$^{1}/_{2}$ cup beef bouillon or broth
$^{1}/_{2}$ cup hot, medium or mild salsa
Flour tortillas

Combine all ingredients in slow cooker and simmer on low for at least 4 hours. Serve wrapped in flour tortillas with your favorite fixings.

David W. Foxworth
APO AE

BREADED VENISON WITH HOLLANDAISE SAUCE

6 pieces venison tenderloin, cut 1-inch thick
   and butterflied
Oil for deep frying
1 egg
1 cup milk
2 cups plain fine breading
1$^{1}/_{2}$ tsp. seasoned salt
2 pkgs. hollandaise sauce mix
8 oz. fresh mushrooms, thinly sliced
Dried parsley (optional)

Heat oil in deep fryer to 375°F. Mix egg and milk in one dish, and mix breading and seasoned salt in another. Prepare hollandaise sauce according to package directions. Keep sauce warm, stirring often to prevent skin forming on top. Dip venison in milk and egg mixture, then in breading. Deep fry 2 minutes for rare, 4$^{1}/_{2}$ minutes for medium and 6 minutes for well done. Set venison aside, keeping warm. Deep fry mushrooms until lightly browned. Place in bowl and lightly season with additional seasoned salt. Serve venison on individual plates, topped with hollandaise sauce and mushrooms and sprinkled with dried parsley if desired.

Curtis Klemann
Saxon, WI

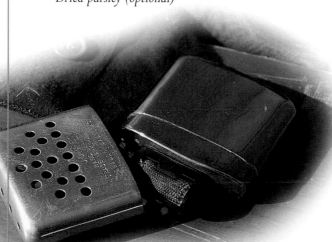

VENISON OVEN STEW

2 lbs. venison (or other big game meat),
    cut into 1-inch cubes
1 tsp. salt
1/4 tsp. pepper
1 tsp. garlic powder
1 tsp. paprika
1 tsp. meat tenderizer (optional)
10-oz. can tomato soup
10-oz. can water
1 T. sugar
2 T. tapioca
2 medium onions, sliced
1 cup chopped celery
2 cups chopped carrots
4 medium potatoes, peeled and cut into large cubes

Place meat in heavy, oven-proof casserole and sprinkle with salt, pepper, garlic powder, paprika and meat tenderizer. Mix tomato soup, water, sugar, tapioca, onions, celery, carrots and potatoes; pour mixture over meat. Cover and bake at 350°F for 4 hours.

Mary Anne Lecce
Collinsville, IL

VENISON CAMP STEW

2 lbs. venison stew meat, finely cubed
2 cups flour
1 T. seasoned salt
1 tsp. ground pepper
1 tsp. spicy no-salt seasoning
1/2 cup olive oil
9 qts. water
4 cans beef broth
10 beef bouillon cubes
3 lbs. potatoes, cubed
2 lbs. carrots, sliced
2 lbs. turnips, cubed
3 ribs celery, sliced
4 medium onions, cubed
1/2 cup chopped fresh parsley

Mix flour, seasoned salt, pepper and no-salt seasoning in a plastic bag. Add cubed venison and shake well. Fry coated meat in olive oil, being careful not to overcook. Transfer meat to 12-quart pot and add water, beef broth, bouillon cubes, potatoes, carrots, turnips, celery, onions and parsley. Slowly bring to a boil. Reduce heat and simmer for 3 to 4 hours.

Joseph Allen
Chester, VT

COUNTRY FRIED VENISON STEAK

4 boneless venison steaks, about 4 oz. each
$^1/_2$ cup flour
$^1/_2$ tsp. salt
$^1/_2$ tsp. pepper
1 cup crushed saltines
$^3/_4$ cup buttermilk
3 T. cooking oil
1 can condensed cream of mushroom soup
1 cup milk

Combine flour, salt and pepper in plastic bag. Place cracker crumbs in separate bag. Pour buttermilk into shallow bowl. Coat steaks in seasoned flour, dip in buttermilk and coat with cracker crumbs. Heat oil in large skillet over medium-high heat, cook steaks for 2 to 3 minutes per side until golden brown. Remove steaks and keep warm. Add soup and milk to skillet and bring to a boil, stirring to loosen browned bits from pan. Serve steaks with gravy and mashed potatoes.

Richard Baker
Lima, OH

STEVE'S VENISON STEAK

6 venison steaks
4 T. butter
1 small onion, diced
2 (4-oz.) cans mushroom stems and pieces
$^1/_4$ cup red wine
$^1/_4$ cup sour cream
1 T. gravy flour or cornstarch
Monterey steak seasoning
2 T. butter

Melt 4 tablespoons butter in large skillet. Add onion and mushrooms and cook until onion is translucent. Add wine and sour cream and stir on medium heat. Slowly stir in gravy flour or cornstarch to thicken sauce. Simmer on low. Sprinkle steak seasoning on both sides of steaks. Melt 2 tablespoons butter in another skillet. Sear steaks on high heat on both sides. Lower heat to medium and complete cooking to desired doneness; they're best at medium rare. Serve steaks covered with sauce.

Stephen Gingras
Lowell, MA

VENISON

DEVILED VENISON CHOPS

3 lbs. venison chops
3/4 cup flour
4 tsp. dry mustard
1 tsp. salt
1/2 tsp. pepper
4 T. shortening
1 medium onion, diced
2 cloves garlic, minced
2 carrots, shredded
15-oz. can crushed tomatoes
1 1/2 T. Worcestershire sauce
2 T. honey (fireweed preferred)

Mix flour, mustard, salt and pepper. Rub flour mixture into chops and let stand at room temperature for 30 minutes. Brown chops in shortening in Dutch oven. Add onion, garlic, carrots, tomatoes, Worcestershire sauce and honey. Cover and bake at 350°F for 1 to 2 hours, until very tender. Serve with mashed potatoes and acorn squash baked with honey.

Andi Flanagan
Seward, AK

DEER JERKY

2 lbs. venison, sliced 1/8- to 1/4-inch thick
1 tsp. liquid wood smoke flavoring
1 T. onion powder
1/3 tsp. garlic powder
1/2 tsp. lemon pepper
1/4 cup soy sauce
1/4 cup Worcestershire sauce
4 drops Tabasco sauce

Mix all ingredients except meat. Cover meat with marinade, coating each piece. Refrigerate for 8 hours or overnight. Place meat on cookie racks and dry on top of wood burning stove or in oven at 125° to 150°F. Store in cool, dry place.

Dennis Morgan
Livonia, NY

EXCELLENT VENISON GOETTA

1 lb. ground venison
2 cups hot water
1 medium onion, finely chopped
1 bay leaf, finely crumbled
$^1/_2$ tsp. coarse black pepper
$1^1/_2$ cups oatmeal
1 tsp. salt
1 tsp. onion powder
$^1/_2$ tsp. thyme
$1^1/_2$ tsp. sage
Dash nutmeg
$^1/_4$ tsp. or more crushed red pepper flakes

Combine venison, hot water and onion in a large skillet. Strip bay leaf from center vein and finely crumble into skillet. Simmer until meat is no longer pink and onion is tender. Add pepper, oatmeal and salt. Stir quickly and cook for 3 minutes. Remove from heat and season with onion powder, thyme, sage, nutmeg and crushed red pepper. Spoon meat mixture into loaf pan sprayed with vegetable oil spray. Let stand until firm. Remove from pan, cut loaf in half and wrap each half in plastic wrap. Freeze one and refrigerate the other. To use, slice meat $^1/_4$-inch thick, coat gently with flour and pan fry in small amount of butter or vegetable oil until browned on each side. Serve with eggs and toast for breakfast or with spinach and eggs on toast for dinner.

Dee Buettgenbach
Wamego, KS

EASY VENISON SPAGHETTI SAUCE

2 lbs. ground venison
29-oz. can tomato purée
7 beef bouillon cubes or venison stock
2 medium onions, thinly sliced
16-oz. pkg. fresh mushrooms, sliced
1 green pepper, chopped
1 red pepper, chopped
5³/4-oz. jar of olives, sliced
¹/3 cup honey
1 tsp. basil
¹/2 tsp. thyme
1¹/2 tsp. parsley
1¹/2 tsp. oregano
2 T. molasses
2 medium cloves garlic, chopped
2 T. lemon juice
¹/2 cup cooking sherry

Mix all ingredients except venison in a 5-quart slow cooker and place on low heat setting. Brown venison in skillet, then add to slow cooker. Cook for about 8 hours on low, stirring occasionally.

Stephen Gingras
Lowell, MA

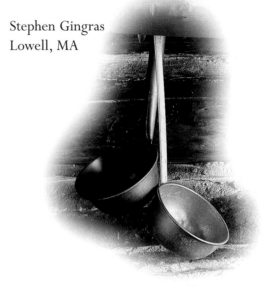

LOUMAN'S MEATLOAF MADNESS

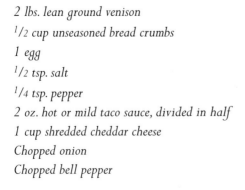

2 lbs. lean ground venison
¹/2 cup unseasoned bread crumbs
1 egg
¹/2 tsp. salt
¹/4 tsp. pepper
2 oz. hot or mild taco sauce, divided in half
1 cup shredded cheddar cheese
Chopped onion
Chopped bell pepper

Combine venison, bread crumbs, egg, salt, pepper and half of taco sauce. On a sheet of wax paper, shape meat mixture into rectangle about ¹/2- to 1-inch thick. Sprinkle cheese, onion and pepper evenly on meat, leaving room at edges. Roll into loaf and place in greased 8 x 12-inch meatloaf pan, seam side down. Top with remaining taco sauce. Bake at 350°F for 1 to 1¹/4 hour.

Eric Lucido
Londonderry, NH

VENISON SANDWICH BARBECUE

1¹/2 lbs. ground venison
1 to 2 T. vegetable oil
1 cup finely chopped celery
1 cup finely chopped onion
1 cup finely chopped bell pepper
¹/4 cup packed light brown sugar
1¹/2 tsp. dry mustard
4 T. chili powder
1¹/4 cups ketchup
1 cup beef broth
1 tsp. vinegar
¹/2 tsp. Worcestershire sauce (optional)
¹/4 tsp. salt
¹/8 tsp. pepper

Cook celery, onion and bell pepper in oil in a large skillet, stirring until tender. Add venison and cook until brown, stirring meat to break up lumps. Add brown sugar, mustard, chili powder, ketchup, broth, vinegar and Worcestershire sauce if desired. Simmer for 30 minutes. Season to taste with salt and pepper. Serve on hamburger buns with a dill pickle and coleslaw.

Ken Proffitt
Reading, OH

VENISON AND RICE CASSEROLE

1 lb. ground venison
¹/2 cup chopped onion
¹/4 cup diced green pepper
1 garlic clove, minced
1 tsp. salt
1 tsp. parsley flakes
2 tsp. dried oregano
2 tsp. dried basil
¹/2 tsp. black pepper
8-oz. can tomato sauce
16-oz. can stewed tomatoes
3 cups cooked rice
16-oz. cream-style cottage cheese
¹/3 cup Parmesan cheese

Prepare rice and set aside. Brown meat in skillet. Add onion, green pepper and garlic. Cook until vegetables are tender. Add salt, parsley, oregano, basil, pepper, tomato sauce and tomatoes. Simmer for 5 minutes. Layer rice, meat sauce and cottage cheese in buttered 3-quart baking dish. Bake at 350°F for 30 minutes. Top with Parmesan cheese and bake 10 minutes longer.

John Tamborella
Milton, FL

Chili Relleno Casserole

CHILI RELLENO CASSEROLE

1 1/2 lbs. ground venison
1/2 onion, chopped
7-oz. can diced green chiles
1 1/2 cups cheddar cheese, shredded
4 eggs, well beaten
1/4 cup flour
1/2 tsp. salt
1/2 cup milk

Brown venison with onion. Place half of meat mixture in 9 x 13-inch baking pan. Layer with half of green chiles and half of cheese, then with remaining chiles and cheese. Combine eggs, flour, salt and milk; mix well. Pour egg mixture over layers and bake at 325°F for 45 minutes.

David W. Foxworth
APO AE

VENISON LASAGNA

1 lbs. ground or shredded venison
1 T. olive oil
1 T. chopped or crushed garlic
1 cup chopped onion
2 cups chopped mushrooms
20-oz. can tomato sauce
2 cups water
16-oz. pkg. lasagna noodles
16 oz. part-skim mozzarella cheese
16 oz. skim ricotta cheese
1 oz. grated Parmesan
1 T. oregano
1 T. sweet basil

Brown venison, garlic, onion and mushrooms in oil until vegetables are tender. Add tomato sauce and water to skillet and bring to a boil. Reduce heat and simmer for 10 minutes. Spray 8 x 14-inch pan with nonstick cooking oil. Cover bottom with sauce and cover with 1 layer of uncooked lasagna noodles. Add layer of sauce, mozzarella, ricotta and Parmesan cheese. Add 2 layers of uncooked noodles and remaining sauce and cheeses. Sprinkle with oregano and sweet basil. Bake at 350°F for 1 hour. Turn oven off and let lasagna stand in oven for 30 minutes. Remove from oven and let stand for another 10 to 20 minutes before serving.

Dennis L. Morgan
Livonia, NY

GROUND VENISON

SUMMER SAUSAGE

5 lbs. ground venison (may substitute 1 lb.
  with hot pork sausage)
5 tsp. curing salt or meat cure
2^1/$_2$ T. mustard seed
2^1/$_2$ tsp. garlic salt
1 T. hickory-smoked salt

Combine all ingredients and mix well. Cover and refrigerate for 4 days, kneading mixture each day. On the 4th day, shape meat mixture into 4 rolls. Place rolls in shallow, flat pan. Bake, uncovered, at 140°F for 8 hours. Cool, wrap and store in refrigerator. Rolls can be frozen until needed. Serve with crackers and top with colby cheese.

Donald R. Smith
Florissant, MO

BOB'S MEATLOAF DELUXE

2 lbs. ground venison
^{3}/$_4$ cup bread crumbs
^{3}/$_4$ cup milk
1 tsp. seasoned salt
^{1}/$_2$ tsp. sweet basil or ^{1}/$_2$ tsp. thyme
1 clove garlic, minced (optional)
^{1}/$_2$ cup chopped onion
2 eggs, slightly beaten
2 to 3 slices bacon (optional)

Combine venison, bread crumbs, milk, seasoned salt, basil or thyme, garlic, onion and eggs. Mix well and form into loaf on 12-inch baking pan with 2^1/$_2$- to 3-inch sides (lined with foil to ease clean-up). Bake at 400°F for 30 minutes; then, if desired, place bacon on top of loaf. Lower temperature to 325°F and bake an additional 45 minutes. Let stand for 10 minutes before serving.

Robert Gross
Vincentown, NJ

VENISON MEATBALL STROGANOFF

2 lbs. ground venison

3^{1}/$_{2}$ cups water

^{1}/$_{2}$ cup seasoned bread crumbs

^{1}/$_{2}$ cup Parmesan cheese

3 tsp. salt

1^{1}/$_{2}$ tsp. pepper

1 small onion, finely chopped

1 rib celery, thinly sliced

2 beef bouillon cubes

^{1}/$_{4}$ cup cornstarch

13^{1}/$_{2}$-oz. can sliced mushrooms, drained

10-oz. can cream of mushroom soup

2 cups sour cream

Mix venison, 1^{1}/$_{4}$ cups water, bread crumbs, Parmesan cheese, 2 teaspoons salt and 1 teaspoon pepper. Roll into 1^{1}/$_{2}$-inch meatballs and place on cookie sheet with sides. Bake at 450°F for 20 minutes. Meanwhile, combine 2 cups water, onion, celery, bouillon cubes, 1 tsp. salt and ^{1}/$_{2}$ tsp. pepper in saucepan, and bring to a boil. Mix ^{1}/$_{4}$ cup of water and cornstarch; stir into saucepan and cook until sauce thickens. Stir in mushrooms, soup and sour cream and mix. Pour over meatballs in casserole dish. Cover and bake at 350°F for 30 minutes. Serve over egg noodles.

Dale Pinto
Crafton, PA

TEXAS VENISON HASH

1 lb. ground venison

1 T. chili powder

1 large onion, sliced

1 large green pepper, sliced

^{1}/$_{2}$ cup rice, uncooked

15^{1}/$_{2}$-oz. can tomatoes

Brown venison with chili powder, onion and green pepper. Combine in casserole dish with rice and tomatoes. Mix well. Cover and bake at 350°F for 1 hour.

David W. Foxworth
APO AE

GROUND VENISON

MOM'S VENISON STICK

5 lbs. ground venison or elk
5 tsp. Morton's Tender Quick salt
2^1/$_2$ tsp. whole mustard seed
1 tsp. celery seed
2^1/$_2$ tsp. pepper
3 tsp. garlic salt
2 T. garlic powder
1 T. onion powder
1 T. liquid smoke flavoring

Mix all ingredients well; cover and refrigerate. Mix each day for 3 days. Form into logs and bake at 225°F for 5 hours. Serve hot or cold. Makes 4 logs about 8 inches long and 1^1/$_2$ inches in diameter.

Tara Mize
Naches, WA

VENISON BIEROKS

1^1/$_2$ lb. ground venison
3 cups cabbage, chopped
1 large onion, chopped
1 tsp. salt
1 T. pepper
3 cans Texas can biscuits
10 oz. shredded mozzarella cheese

Brown venison. Add cabbage and onion to skillet, cover and cook over low heat for about 15 minutes or until thoroughly heated. Add salt and pepper. Roll biscuits out to about ^{1}/$_8$- to ^{1}/$_4$-inch thick. Place a layer of cheese, a portion of meat and cabbage mixture, and another layer of cheese on biscuit. Lay another biscuit on top and pinch edges together to seal, forming a little package. Place on lightly greased cookie sheet and bake at 350°F for 15 to 20 minutes or until biscuits are brown.

Kevin J. Keeler
Moncks Corner, SC

RUSSIAN VENISON
DUMPLING APPETIZERS

1 lb. ground venison
1 onion, minced
2 cloves garlic, minced
Salt and freshly ground pepper
3 pickled beets, chopped (optional)
2 cups flour
1 egg, beaten
1 tsp. salt
$^2/_3$ cup ice water
$^1/_4$ cup butter, melted
$^1/_4$ cup fine mustard
$^1/_4$ cup white wine vinegar

Brown venison, onion and garlic; season with salt and pepper. Drain. Mix in beets if desired. Combine flour, salt and egg and gradually add water to make dough. Knead until dough becomes elastic. Roll $^1/_3$ of dough at a time into very thin sheet and cut into 2-inch squares. Place a scant teaspoon of meat onto square and fold into triangle. Seal edges with a floured fork. Place on floured cookie sheet until all are formed into dumplings. Cover with damp paper towels to keep from drying out. Drop a few at a time into large kettle of boiling water, stirring to keep from sticking. Boil for about 10 minutes or just until tender. Drizzle with melted butter and serve with mustard and vinegar blended together into sauce.

Andi Flanagan
Seward, AK

GROUND VENISON

VENISON-FILLED PEPPERS

1 lb. ground venison
4 to 5 medium green peppers
1 onion, diced
Salt and pepper
1 1/2 cups rice, cooked
Taco seasoning
1 can refried beans
3 cups shredded cheddar cheese
Salsa

Core and wash whole peppers and set aside. Brown venison and onion in large skillet and season with salt and pepper. While meat is browning, cook rice in small pot. When meat is browned, add taco seasoning, refried beans and just enough water to dissolve seasoning. When heated through, add rice and simmer until thick. Place peppers in a meatloaf pan and spoon meat mixture into peppers, filling no more than half full. Sprinkle about 1/4 inch of cheddar cheese on meat and finish stuffing peppers with meat. Spoon any excess meat mixture around outside of peppers. Sprinkle peppers with remaining cheddar cheese and place in preheated oven at 300°F for 1 hour, watching to make sure cheese doesn't burn. Cover with your favorite salsa and serve.

Thomas Bruni
Gleason, WI

VENISON ITALIAN PASTA

2 lbs. ground venison
1 large sweet onion, chopped
4 (29-oz.) cans crushed tomatoes
3 T. basil
2 tsp. fennel seed
1 cup bread crumbs
2 eggs
1 tsp. granulated garlic
3 T. Parmesan cheese

In large kettle, sauté onion in olive oil until translucent. Add tomatoes, basil and fennel and cook over low heat for several hours. Mix bread crumbs, eggs, garlic and Parmesan cheese with venison and shape into 32 meatballs. Bake at 350°F for 35 minutes. Add to sauce and simmer for 1 hour. Serve over your favorite pasta.

Ray J. Lear III
Watertown, NY

VENISON-FILLED PEPPERS

WHITETAIL TACO SOUP

2 lbs. ground venison
10-oz. can diced tomatoes with green chiles
1 can tomatoes
1 can yellow hominy
1 can white hominy
1 can ranch-style beans
1 pkg. taco mix
1 pkg. ranch dressing mix
2 tsp. garlic powder
1 tsp. dill weed
$^1/_2$ tsp. cayenne pepper (optional)
4 green onions, chopped
2 cups shredded cheese (cheddar or colby and Monterey Jack cheese blend)
$^1/_2$ cup sliced or diced ripe olives
$^1/_2$ cup sliced green olives
Sour cream (optional)

Brown ground venison and drain fat. Add tomatoes, both cans of hominy, beans, taco mix, ranch dressing mix, garlic powder, dill weed and cayenne pepper. Stir and heat over medium heat for 15 to 20 minutes. Top each serving with chopped onions, shredded cheese, olives and sour cream. Serve with tortilla chips or corn bread on the side.

Rob Wodzinski
Iron River, MI

GROUND VENISON

MEXICAN MEATLOAF

1^1/$_2$ lbs. ground venison
^{1}/$_3$ crushed tortilla chips
^{1}/$_3$ cup chopped green pepper
15-oz. can tomato sauce
^{1}/$_2$ cup chopped onion
1 pkg. taco seasoning mix

Reserve 1 cup of tomato sauce. Combine all other ingredients and mix well. Spoon mixture into 9 x 5-inch loaf pan. Bake at 350°F for 1 to 1^1/$_4$ hours. Heat reserved tomato sauce and serve with meatloaf.

David W. Foxworth
APO AE

VENISON MANICOTTI

8 oz. ground venison
8 oz. mild Italian sausage
14 manicotti noodles
8 saltine crackers
Sage
Oregano
Garlic powder
8 oz. shredded mozzarella cheese
4 eggs
^{1}/$_4$ cup Parmesan cheese
Salt and pepper
14-oz. jar spaghetti sauce

Boil noodles for 8 minutes and drain. Brown venison and sausage and remove from heat. Crush crackers and season with pinch of sage, oregano and garlic powder. Mix 4 oz. mozzarella cheese, eggs, cracker mixture, Parmesan cheese, salt and pepper and about half of the spaghetti sauce. Mix well. Pour just enough of remaining sauce into 13 x 9-inch baking pan to line bottom. Using a small spoon, fill noodles well with meat mixture. Place noodles in pan and pour the last of the spaghetti sauce over filled noodles, spreading sauce evenly with spoon. Top with remaining mozzarella and, if desired, more Parmesan cheese. Cover with foil and bake at 350°F for 45 minutes. Serve with garlic toast.

Ronald D. Binning
Texarkana, TX

GROUND VENISON

Sweet 'n Sour Meatballs

1 to 2 lbs. lean ground venison or elk
8-oz. can water chestnuts, drained and chopped
2 eggs
$^1/_3$ cup dry bread crumbs
1 T. Worcestershire sauce
4 tsp. instant beef bouillon

Sauce

1 cup water
$^1/_2$ cup brown sugar, firmly packed
$^1/_2$ cup lemon juice
$^1/_4$ cup ketchup
2 T. cornstarch
$^1/_4$ tsp. salt
1 large onion, chopped (optional)
1 tsp. cayenne pepper (optional)
1 cup chopped mushrooms (optional)
1 large red or green pepper, cut into 1-inch squares
Chopped parsley (optional)
3 jalapeño peppers, chopped (optional)

In a large bowl, combine meat, water chestnuts, eggs, bread crumbs, Worcestershire sauce and bouillon. Mix well. Shape into 1$^1/_4$-inch meatballs and brown in oil in a large skillet. Remove meatballs from pan and pour off fat.

For sauce: In the same skillet, combine water, brown sugar, lemon juice, ketchup, cornstarch, salt, onion, mushrooms and cayenne pepper. Mix well and cook over medium heat, stirring until sauce thickens. Reduce heat, add meatballs and simmer, uncovered, for 10 minutes. Add peppers and heat through. Garnish with parsley if desired. Refrigerate leftovers.

Richard D. Buth
Oconomowoc, WI

GROUND VENISON

BOBOTIE
(PRONOUNCED BOW-BOO-TEA)

2^1/4 lbs. ground venison
2 medium onions
2 T. sunflower oil
1 T. curry powder
1 tsp. turmeric
2 T. white vinegar or lemon juice
1 T. sugar
1 tsp. salt
^{1}/2 tsp. black pepper
2 slices white bread with crusts removed
1 cup milk
2 large eggs
2^1/2 oz. raisins
3 T. fruit chutney
Grated rind of 1 lemon (optional)
2 bay leaves
6 to 12 almonds, blanched and quartered
6 lemon leaves

Parboil whole onions until opaque. Remove onions and reserve water in pan. Peel and thinly slice onions; fry and chop onion slices in sunflower oil until golden. Add curry powder and turmeric; fry for 2 minutes, stirring constantly. Add vinegar or lemon juice, sugar, salt and pepper. In the meantime, soak bread in milk, squeeze dry, strain milk and set milk aside. Crumble ground venison into a large skillet, adding onion water and a little boiling water; cook for 5 minutes. Lightly mix meat, bread, onion mixture and 1 egg, raisins, chutney and lemon rind. Pack meat mixture into buttered casserole and add bay leaves.

Cover and bake for 1^1/2 hours at 350°F. Remove from oven and stick almonds and lemon leaves (made into cone shapes) into meat. Add enough milk to reserved milk to make 1 full cup; whip milk and 1 egg. Carefully pour milk and egg across backside of spoon over meat. Return dish to oven, reduce heat to 300°F. Bake uncovered for 30 minutes. Serve this South African dish with fluffy white rice and fresh vegetables or a crisp green salad.

Peter Bird
Upper Hutt, New Zealand

GROUND VENISON

Mom's Hawaiian Venison Meatballs

1 lb. ground venison
1 lb. breakfast sausage
2 eggs
2 T. milk
$^1/_2$ cup rolled oats
1 small onion, diced
Seasoned salt
Pepper

Sauce

20-oz. can pineapple chunks
15$^1/_4$-oz. can peaches
1 cup sugar
2 T. cornstarch
$^3/_4$ cup vinegar
1 T. soy sauce
$^1/_4$ tsp. ginger
1 chicken bouillon cube
1 green pepper, diced

Mix venison, sausage, eggs, milk, oats, onion, seasoned salt and pepper. Lightly coat skillet with cooking spray. Shape mixture into 1$^1/_2$-inch meatballs and fry slowly until fully cooked. For sauce, drain pineapple and peaches into a bowl or a 2-cup measuring cup; add water to make 1$^1/_2$ cups liquid. Set fruit aside. In saucepan, combine fruit liquid, sugar, cornstarch, vinegar, soy sauce, ginger and bouillon cube. Bring to a boil, stirring constantly. When sauce is thickened, pour over meatballs and simmer for 30 minutes. Add pineapple, peaches and green pepper and simmer another 30 minutes.

Thomas Wieling
Holland, MI

GROUND VENISON

CHAPTER 3

UPLAND GAME BIRDS

P heasant, grouse from both forest and prairie, quail,
chukar, huns … upland game birds present both hunting
joy and eating pleasure.

What could be finer than walking up a pheasant on an
October morning, marching across the prairie for sharptails, following a brace of pointers in the quail meadows,
or wandering the popple chasing grouse on a glorious
Indian summer afternoon?

One thing comes close, real close: eating the birds you
are fortunate enough to bring home, especially when they
are prepared well. Each one is a reason for celebration, and
we present here the recipe ideas you need to pull off the
feast famously—celebrating both the hunt and the delica-
cies in your pot, skillet or pan, or on your spit.

"A Morning Double–Ruffed Grouse" by David A. Maass.
Courtesy of the artist and WildWings Inc., Lake City, MN 55041.
(800) 445-4833.

WESTON CANYON GROUSE

2 sharptails or ruffs, cleaned and whole
   (or 2 chukars, 4 quail, 1 big
   blue grouse or 1 pheasant)
1/2 cup flour
1 tsp. garlic salt
1 tsp. salt
2 tsp. crushed rosemary
2 tsp. thyme
1 tsp. sage
1 tsp. ground black or mixed pepper
1/2 tsp. paprika
1/2 cup olive oil
4 T. butter
3 cloves garlic, minced

Remove all meat from birds and cut into bite-sized chunks 1 to 2 inches long. Mix flour, garlic salt, salt, rosemary, thyme, sage, pepper and paprika together. Roll meat in seasoned flour to coat thoroughly. Heat olive oil and butter in large cast iron or heavy skillet. Cook minced garlic for about 30 seconds. Add meat and sauté for about 7 or 8 minutes, stirring constantly until browned and a little crusty.

Serve with French bread or focaccia, a mixed green salad and a good wine.

Tom Carpenter
Plymouth, MN

JALAPEÑO-PHEASANT APPETIZERS

1 to 2 pheasant breasts
24 jalapeño peppers
1 cup shredded cheddar cheese
8-oz. pkg. cream cheese
12 slices bacon, cut in half

Slice partially frozen pheasant breast meat 1/4-inch thick and 1-inch wide. Seed peppers, keeping them whole. Combine cheddar and cream cheeses and stuff jalapeños. Wrap pheasant slices around jalapeños and then wrap with bacon. Secure with toothpick. Broil, turning frequently until bacon is crisped and done.

Dee Buettgenbach
Wamego, KS

IOWA PHEASANT CASSEROLE

2 pheasants, cooked and cubed
4 to 6 slices bread, diced or crumbled
$^1/_4$ cup butter
2 (10-oz.) pkgs. frozen broccoli
   (or broccoli-cauliflower mixture)
2 (10$^1/_2$-oz.) cans cream of mushroom soup
$^1/_2$ cup mayonnaise
$^1/_2$ cup sour cream
1 tsp. lemon juice
$^1/_2$ tsp. curry powder (optional)
$^1/_2$ to 1 cup grated sharp cheese

Bake pheasant at 350°F for 35 minutes, remove meat from bones and cube. Brown bread cubes or crumbs in butter and set aside. Cook frozen vegetables for 5 minutes, drain and arrange in shallow casserole dish. Place pheasant over broccoli. Combine soup, mayonnaise, sour cream, lemon juice and curry powder in saucepan and heat. Pour mixture over vegetables and pheasant and sprinkle with buttered bread crumbs and grated cheese. Bake at 325°F for 25 to 30 minutes (350°F if using metal pan).

Curt Larson
North English, IA

GROUSE CASHEW STIR-FRY

Grouse breasts
1 T. extra virgin olive oil
1 T. minced garlic
2 (16-oz.) bags frozen stir-fry
   vegetables, defrosted
4 oz. stir-fry sauce
8 oz. cashews, chopped
1 lb. long-grain rice, cooked

Debone and chop grouse breasts into $^1/_2$-inch chunks. Place in wok or large skillet with hot olive oil and garlic and cook on high heat until meat is golden brown at edges. Add thawed vegetables and cook until heated through. Add stir-fry sauce and chopped cashews. Cook about 2 minutes on medium heat. Serve over hot rice.

Ken Blay Jr.
East Burke, VT

PHEASANT IN WILD RICE

2 to 4 pheasant breasts, boned
White rice or wild rice
Powdered onion soup mix
2 cans cream of mushroom soup (or cream
    of celery or cream of chicken soup)

Butter bottom and sides of roasting pan and sprinkle with desired amount of rice for number of people to be served. Add pheasant breasts and sprinkle with onion soup mix. Add 2 cans of cream-style soup. Add liquid according to rice package directions, subtracting to allow for 2 cans of soup. If rice soaks up too much liquid during cooking, add water as needed. Bake at 350°F for 1 hour or longer for larger meals. Works with rabbit, squirrel, duck, goose or other small game. If meat is tough, brown prior to baking.

Tully E. Kessler
Knoxville, TN

SIMMERED SAGE HEN

5- to 8-lb. sage hen (sage grouse)
Flour
Salt and pepper
Cooking oil
2 cans beer

Cut sage hen into serving pieces, slicing breasts to 1/2-inch thickness. Create mixture of flour, salt and pepper. Coat meat in flour mixture; brown in oil in cast iron skillet. When thoroughly browned, pour in beer. Cover, reduce heat and simmer for 30 to 45 minutes. Remove meat from liquid and serve.

Ken Stine
Sparks, NV

Baked Turkey and Macaroni

2 cups cooked and diced turkey breast

2 cups cooked macaroni

1 onion, diced

$^1/_2$ bell pepper, diced

$^1/_2$ tsp. pepper

1 T. lemon juice

1 can cream of mushroom soup

2 cups grated cheddar cheese

Prepare macaroni according to package directions. Mix turkey breast, macaroni, onion, bell pepper, ground pepper, lemon juice and soup in a large bowl. Pour mixture into casserole dish, cover and bake at 350°F for 30 minutes. Remove cover, top dish with cheddar cheese and continue baking uncovered until cheese melts.

Kenneth W. Crummett
Sugar Grove, WV

Turkey Dressing

10 cups bread crumbs

1 tsp. poultry seasoning

$^1/_8$ tsp. sage

2 tsp. salt

$^1/_2$ tsp. black pepper

Pinch garlic powder

3 cups chopped celery

$^1/_2$ onion, chopped

$1^1/_2$ qts. chicken broth or turkey juices

Put bread crumbs in large bread bowl. Add seasonings, celery and onion and stir in broth. Bake at 350°F for 45 to 60 minutes. Stuff turkey and roast bird as usual.

John Tamborella
Milton, FL

TEN-MINUTE DOVES

12 to 15 doves
1/2 cup chicken broth
2 T. soy sauce
1 tsp. ground ginger
3 tsp. fresh orange juice
2 1/2 tsp. chopped salted peanuts (optional)
2 tsp. butter
1/3 cup thinly sliced celery
2/3 cup thinly sliced carrots
1/2 cup or more diced onion

Rinse doves, drain and dry very, very well (the trick to braising any bird, but especially dove, is thorough drying). Combine broth, soy sauce, ginger, orange juice and peanuts in a bowl and set aside. Melt butter in a 10-inch skillet over medium-high heat. Reduce heat and sauté celery, carrots and onion for 5 minutes. Add liquid mixture to pan and simmer. Put thoroughly dry doves in pan, cover and cook for 10 minutes. This recipe goes against the common practice of browning doves before cooking, but it captures the true flavor of this wonderful game bird.

Angel Roche
Miami, FL

TENNESSEE GRILLED DOVE

3 to 4 dove breasts per person
Italian dressing
1 small piece jalapeño pepper per breast
1 strip bacon per breast

Remove breast bone from dove and place meat in pan or bowl. Pour Italian dressing over breast meat and marinate overnight. Drain and pat meat dry. Place 1 small piece of jalapeño pepper in center of breast, wrap with 1 strip of bacon and secure with toothpick. Grill until bacon strip is done.

Randy Tarpley
Brush Creek, TN

DEE'S FAVORITE PHEASANT

1 pheasant, cut into serving pieces
1 cup flour
1/2 tsp. salt
1/4 tsp. pepper
1/2 tsp. garlic powder
1 tsp. poultry seasoning
1/2 cup vegetable oil for frying
1 small onion, diced
1 can cream of mushroom soup
Bay leaves (optional)

Combine flour, salt, pepper, garlic powder and poultry seasoning and dredge pheasant. Heat vegetable oil in heavy skillet and fry pheasant until lightly browned. Place pheasant pieces in large casserole. Combine 1/3 cup dredging flour, 1 1/2 cups cold water, onion, mushroom soup and bay leaves. Pour over pheasant. Bake at 350°F for 1 1/2 hours or until very tender.

Dee Buettgenbach
Wamego, KS

ROAST WILD TURKEY

Wild turkey, cleaned
1 large marinade injector
1 bottle Italian dressing
2 cloves crushed garlic
1/3 cup dry white wine or water
2 T. lemon juice
1 lb. turkey bacon
Roasting bag

Mix Italian dressing, garlic, white wine and lemon juice to make marinade. Inject turkey with marinade in several places in breast, thighs and legs. Place turkey in large plastic bag and refrigerate overnight. Remove turkey from bag and arrange turkey bacon on breast and thighs, securing with toothpicks. Place bird in roasting bag (stuffed if desired) and roast at 325°F for 4 to 5 hours or until meat thermometer reads 185°F.

Richard Baker
Lima, OH

NINE-TO-FIVE GROUSE OR PHEASANT

2 to 4 grouse or pheasant breasts
1 can cream of chicken soup
6 to 12 slices thick-sliced bacon
1 cup milk

Pour cream of chicken soup into slow cooker. Wrap bacon around grouse or pheasant breasts and set in slow cooker. Cook on low heat for at least 8 hours. In last hour of cooking, add milk to slow cooker. Serve over rice.

Kurt Amundson
Long Prairie, MN

CAPTAIN'S COUNTRY DOVE OR PHEASANT BREASTS

12 dove breasts (or 4 pheasant or chicken breasts)
2 T. flour
1/2 tsp. salt
1/8 tsp. pepper
2 T. butter
1/4 cup chopped onion
1/4 cup chopped green pepper
1 clove garlic, minced
1 tsp. curry powder
1/2 tsp. salt
1/4 tsp. thyme
16-oz. can stewed tomatoes
2 T. seedless raisins

Combine flour, salt and pepper in a bag with dove or pheasant breasts and toss to mix. Melt butter in skillet and brown meat on all sides. Remove meat, setting it aside. In skillet, sauté onion, green pepper and garlic with curry powder, salt and thyme until onion and green pepper are tender. Add tomatoes and simmer, uncovered, for 10 minutes. Return meat to skillet and add raisins. Cover and simmer for about 40 minutes until tender. Serve with rice.

Mary Anne Lecce
Collinsville, IL

Pheasant with Leeks and Pears

2^{1}/$_{2}$- to 3-lb. pheasant
3 medium leeks (white parts only), thinly sliced
6 scallions, trimmed and finely chopped
4 thin slices prosciutto, chopped
1 medium parsnip, peeled, chopped
1 medium pear, peeled, cored, sliced
1^{1}/$_{2}$ cups champagne or dry white wine
1 T. olive oil
1 tsp. salt
1 tsp. pepper
1 T. fresh parsley, chopped

In small bowl, mix 1^{1}/$_{2}$ leeks with scallions and prosciutto and set aside. Carefully insert finger under pheasant skin at neck, creating a space between breast meat and skin. Repeat at other end, below ribs. With sharp knife, make 2 or 3 slits in skin and flesh of both legs on all sides. Stuff as much of leek mixture as possible under skin and into slits. Combine any excess mixture with remaining leeks. Add parsnip and pear to leek mixture and stuff inside pheasant cavity. Pour champagne or wine into cavity and truss bird with butcher's twine or stuffing skewers. Place pheasant in large roasting pan and pour remaining champagne or wine over bird. Rub skin with olive oil and sprinkle with salt, pepper and parsley. Cover and roast at 350°F for about 1 hour. Remove cover and baste; bake, uncovered, for another 30 minutes or until meat thermometer inserted in drumstick flesh registers 160°F. Serve with pan drippings and leek mixture ladled over meat.

William S. Soltis
Saginaw, MI

UPLAND GAME BIRDS

JASON'S PEPPER-CHEESE DOVE

UPLAND GAME BIRDS

15 to 20 doves
10 slices hot pepper cheese
10 to 15 slices bacon

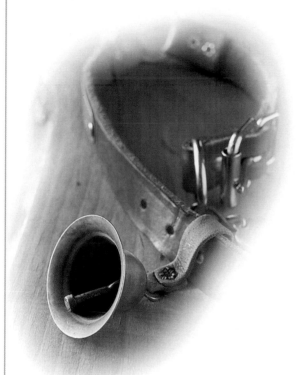

Fillet meat from breast bone and cut each slice into 3 or 4 pieces. If desired, season with favorite seasonings. Place hot pepper cheese between 2 slices of fillet, wrap in bacon and secure with toothpick. Place on grill and cook until done.

Jason Renaud
Charleston, MO

TURKEY PIE

2 cups cooked, diced turkey
4^1/$_2$-oz. jar sliced mushrooms, drained
^{1}/$_2$ cup sliced green onions
^{1}/$_2$ tsp. salt
1 cup shredded natural Swiss cheese
1^1/$_2$ cups milk
3 eggs
^{3}/$_4$ cup baking mix

Heat oven to 400°F. Grease 10-inch pie plate and fill with turkey, mushrooms, onions, salt and cheese. Beat milk, eggs and baking mix until smooth; pour over food in pan. Bake for 30 minutes or until knife inserted comes out clean. Cool for 5 minutes before serving.

Eric Withrow
Elkview, WV

DOVE BREAST PIQUANT

12 dove breasts (or 1¹/₂ lbs. red meat)
2 cups dry red wine
¹/₂ cup olive oil
¹/₂ cup soy sauce
¹/₄ cup firmly packed light brown sugar
2 tsp. ground ginger
1 tsp. dried oregano, crumbled
1 clove garlic, minced
8 oz. fresh mushrooms, sliced

Arrange dove breasts (or red meat) in large, shallow nonaluminum baking dish. Mix wine, olive oil, soy sauce, brown sugar, ginger, oregano and garlic; pour marinade over meat. Cover and refrigerate for at least 2 hours or overnight. (If using red meat, brown in 2 T. olive oil before proceeding.) Transfer meat and marinade to large oven-proof skillet. Bake, uncovered, in marinade for about 40 minutes, basting twice. Transfer skillet to stove top, add mushrooms and simmer for 15 to 20 minutes over medium heat. Thicken sauce with paste of flour and water. Serve over rice or noodles.

Mary Anne Lecce
Collinsville, IL

GRILLED DOVE

Dove
Italian dressing
1 onion, cut into ¹/₂-inch pieces
Jalapeño peppers, cored and sliced ¹/₂-inch thick
Bacon
Barbecue sauce

Breast and clean birds and marinate in Italian dressing for about 8 hours. Make a ¹/₂-inch cut on both sides of backbone. Place a slice of onion in 1 cut, a jalapeño in the other. Wrap with bacon. Place 4 or 5 on skewer and grill, basting just before done with barbecue sauce.

James Brown, Alvin Tolliver and Jason Stottlemire
Duncanville, TX

Sweet-and-Sour Grilled Quail Breast

Quail or dove breasts
Seasoned salt
Seasoned pepper
Garlic powder
Barbecue spice blend
1 fresh peach slice for each breast
1 slice bacon for each breast

Prepare White Wine Baste (below) and set aside. Season birds with seasoned salt, seasoned pepper, garlic powder and spice blend; place a fresh peach slice in each cavity. Wrap 1 slice uncooked bacon around each breast and secure with toothpick. Grill birds for about 20 minutes over indirect heat, basting with White Wine Baste to keep moist.

Prepare Sweet-and-Sour Peach Glaze (below). About 5 to 10 minutes before birds are done, begin glazing with Sweet-and-Sour Peach Glaze. Brush glaze on at least twice, turning birds between glazing.

White Wine Baste

1 cup water
$^1/_2$ tsp. ground ginger
$^1/_2$ tsp. garlic powder
1 cup dry white wine

Simmer water with ginger and garlic powder until spices are dissolved. Add white wine and stir to blend.

Sweet-and-Sour Peach Glaze

18-oz. jar peach preserves or 1 fresh peach, pitted but not peeled
$^1/_4$ cup red wine vinegar
3 to 4 cloves garlic, minced
1 tsp. ground ginger
1 fresh jalapeño pepper (optional)

Purée peach(es) and, if desired, seeded jalapeño. Combine vinegar, garlic and ginger with peach mixture. Simmer mixture in saucepan to blend and dissolve spices.

Mary Anne Lecce
Collinsville, IL

WILD TURKEY SOUP

STOCK

Leftover wild turkey bones and neck
3 qts. water
3 bay laurel leaves
6 black peppercorns
2 tsp. salt
1 tsp. thyme
6 cloves
¹/₂ tsp. parsley
¹/₄ tsp. liquid smoke flavoring

SOUP

2 to 3 lbs. wild turkey meat, deboned
2 lbs. carrots, sliced
2 medium onions, thinly sliced
2 pkgs. celery
18 oz. fresh baby mushrooms
16-oz. pkg. frozen baby peas
16-oz. pkg. flat egg noodles

Boil stock ingredients in a large stock pot for 4 hours. Continue adding additional water as needed. Remove all bones from stock. Add all soup ingredients except noodles. Cook soup on high for 1 hour and 30 minutes, stirring frequently. Add noodles and cook until noodles are done, about 30 minutes.

Stephen Gingras
Lowell, MA

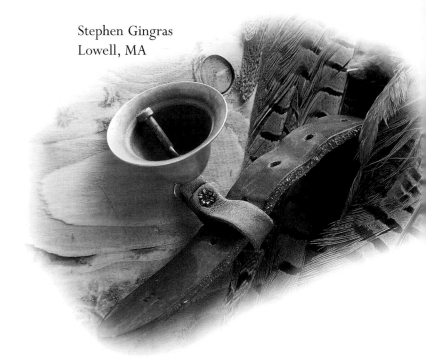

BACON DOVES

6 dove breasts
Bacon
Italian dressing

Place doves in a nonaluminum dish of salt water, refrigerating for half a day. Rinse doves, then wrap each dove breast in bacon, securing bacon with a toothpick. Pour Italian dressing over meat and place on grill. Cook until done.

Chad Wilson
Woodland, AL

DEEP-FRIED CAJUN TURKEY

12-lb. fresh wild turkey
³/4 cup thyme
³/4 cup paprika
¹/4 tsp. salt
¹/4 cup garlic powder
¹/4 cup onion powder
¹/4 cup ground white pepper
¹/4 cup ground black pepper
16-oz. jar Cajun injector with
    injectable marinade
4 to 5 gallons peanut oil

Combine seasonings in bowl. Prepare Cajun marinade according to package directions. Remove giblets and neck from turkey and set aside. Rinse turkey with cold water. Drain cavity well and fill with half of seasoning mixture and marinade. Inject remaining marinade into turkey breast several times, and into thighs and drumsticks. Cover turkey and refrigerate for 8 hours. Rub turkey with remaining seasoning mixture and drain cavity well. Pour oil into deep propane turkey fryer and heat to 350°F according to manufacturer's instructions. Place turkey on fryer rod and carefully lower into hot oil with rod attachment. Fry for 45 minutes.

Joey Goff
Opelika, AL

MARY'S FAMOUS PHEASANT CASSEROLE

3 cups cooked pheasant, cubed
Stuffing mix
¹/2 cup diced onion
¹/2 cup diced celery
1 cup sliced mushrooms
Butter
¹/2 cup mayonnaise
1 can cream of chicken soup
1 egg
¹/2 cup milk
1¹/2 cups shredded mozzarella cheese
1 can Durkee Onions

Prepare stuffing according to package directions and spread in 9 x 13-inch pan. Sauté diced onion, celery and mushrooms in butter. Mix with pheasant and mayonnaise and spread over stuffing. Mix soup, egg and milk and pour over pheasant mix. Bake at 350°F for 40 minutes. Sprinkle with cheese and canned onions and bake for another 15 to 20 minutes.

Mary Mullvain
Duluth, MN

PARTRIDGE STIR-FRY

2 breasts of partridge
Olive oil
Salt and pepper
Garlic, minced or powdered
Parsley
1 T. lemon juice
3 carrots, cut into strips
1 medium onion, cut into pieces
1 small zucchini, sliced
$^1/_2$ head of cauliflower or broccoli,
    cut into pieces
$^1/_2$ red pepper, cut into pieces
$^1/_2$ green pepper, cut into pieces
$^1/_2$ yellow pepper, cut into pieces
2 cups rice

Cut partridge into strips and brown in olive oil over medium heat. Add salt, pepper, garlic, parsley, other favorite spices, herbs or seasonings and lemon juice. Cook until meat is tender. Cook vegetables in separate large skillet over medium heat until tender. Mix meat and vegetables together and simmer for 10 to 15 minutes at very low heat. Serve on a bed of rice.

John W. Larabie
Griffith, Ontario, Canada

BEER DOVE BREASTS

12 dove breasts (or 4 pheasant breasts)
2 T. butter
1 medium onion, chopped
10-oz. can tomato soup
$^2/_3$ cup beer
1 tsp. curry powder
$^1/_2$ tsp. dried oregano, crumbled
Dash of pepper
$^1/_4$ cup grated Parmesan cheese

Sauté onion in butter until tender but not brown. Stir in tomato soup, beer, curry powder, oregano and pepper and simmer uncovered for 10 minutes. Arrange meat in baking dish and pour sauce over meat. Bake uncovered at 350°F for 50 to 55 minutes. Sprinkle with grated cheese and serve with rice.

Mary Anne Lecce
Collinsville, IL

UPLAND GAME BIRDS

Yukon Gold

3 lbs. ptarmigan breasts
2 cups flour
$1/2$ cup butter or margarine
1 medium onion, diced
2 ribs celery, sliced
3 cloves garlic, minced
3 T. flour
$2^1/2$ cups chicken or ptarmigan stock
1 T. curry powder, or more to taste
1 tsp. salt
1 large barely ripe banana, diced
$1/2$ cup cashews

Roll ptarmigan in 2 cups of flour. Brown breasts in butter or margarine in large skillet. Remove meat from skillet and set aside. Add onion, celery and garlic and cook for about 5 minutes. Stir in 3 tablespoons of flour and cook for 1 minute, stirring constantly. Add stock, curry powder and salt. Return ptarmigan to skillet and add banana and cashews. Lower heat, cover and simmer for 45 minutes, stirring occasionally. Serve with rice.

Andi Flanagan
Seward, AK

Barbecued Pheasant

2 whole pheasants
$1/2$ cup water
1 small onion, chopped
2 tsp. Worcestershire sauce
2 chicken bouillon cubes
18-oz. bottle barbecue sauce
$1/2$ cup ketchup

Place pheasants in slow cooker. Add onion, Worcestershire sauce and bouillon cubes and cook on high for 3 to 4 hours. Remove pheasant and drain. Cool and remove bones. Return meat to slow cooker, cooking on low setting for at least 8 hours. Add barbecue sauce and ketchup. Serve on buns.

Lewis Drullinger and Jody Brown
Woodston, KS

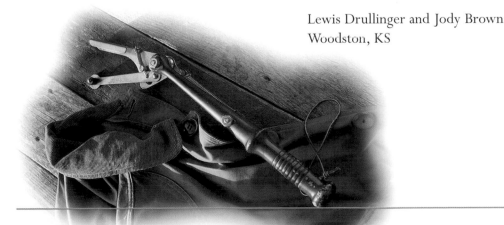

GRILLED QUAIL WITH MANGO AND PEACH SALSA

4 quail
1 medium red onion, chopped (about 1 cup)
1 mango, diced (about 1^1/4 cup)
2 fresh peaches, diced (about 1^1/4 cup)
^{1}/2 cup cilantro, stemmed and finely chopped
3 scallions, chopped (including all but 1 inch of greens)
^{1}/4 cup lime juice
^{1}/2 tsp. hot pepper sauce
2 T. tamari or low sodium soy sauce
1 T. extra virgin olive oil
1 T. ground cumin
1 lime, cut into wedges

Combine onion, mango, peaches, cilantro, scallions, lime juice, pepper sauce, tamari, olive oil and cumin. Mix well and set aside at room temperature for about 1 hour. Start charcoal grill. Wash quail and pat dry. Using scissors or knife, cut back and flatten birds with back of heavy knife or plate. When coals are gray and hot, lay quail on top rack. Grill for 6 to 8 minutes or until lightly browned. Turn and grill for another 4 to 5 minutes or until juices run clear when bird is pierced with knife. Transfer to warm plates, spoon generous portion of salsa over each plate and serve immediately with lime wedges.

William S. Soltis
Saginaw, MI

SPRUCE HEN AND WHITE BEAN CHILI

4 to 5 spruce hen breasts, cut into
*   1^1/$_2$-inch pieces*
1 lb. small white beans, soaked overnight
*   and drained*
2 medium onions, chopped
4 cups chicken broth
3 T. chili powder
1^1/$_2$ T. ground cumin
2 tsp. minced garlic
1 T. sweet paprika
^{1}/$_2$ tsp. salt
^{1}/$_2$ tsp. coarsely ground pepper
7-oz. can diced green chiles
1 jalapeño pepper, minced

Place meat, beans and onions in a large Dutch oven. In a separate bowl, mix broth, chili powder, cumin, garlic, paprika, salt, pepper, green chiles and jalapeño. Pour mixture over contents in Dutch oven; stir. Cook at 325°F for 3 hours. Serve with rice and beer.

Andi Flanagan
Seward, AK

TURKEY IN THE SACK

Turkey
Double-strength brown paper bag
Cooking oil
Seasonings

Oil turkey and season with your favorite herbs and spices, such as rosemary and thyme or basil, oregano and garlic. Oil brown bag and slide turkey into bag, folding and stapling bag opening. Check bag for holes; place on rack in large broiler pan in 325°F-oven. Bake for 20 to 22 minutes per pound if turkey is 12 pounds or under, 16 to 18 minutes per pound if turkey is 13 pounds or more. When turkey is done, poke holes in bag, letting juices run out into a saucepan. Remove turkey from bag and let rest for 30 minutes. Meanwhile, blend some flour and water in a separate dish; add to juices for gravy. Cook gravy until thick and bubbly.

John Tamborella
Milton, FL

UPLAND GAME BIRDS

BRAD'S GAME BIRD DIVAN

2 cups cooked, diced game bird
10-oz. pkg. crouton-style seasoned stuffing mix
14-oz. can chicken broth
^{1}/4 cup butter
8 oz. chopped frozen broccoli
4 oz. shredded cheddar and Monterey Jack cheese blend
1 cup White Sauce (below)

Empty stuffing mix into large bowl and set aside. Heat broth and butter in saucepan until butter is melted. Pour over stuffing and stir quickly to moisten. Spread stuffing in greased 9 x 13-inch baking dish. Distribute game bird evenly over stuffing. Cover game bird layer with chopped broccoli. Prepare White Sauce and pour evenly over game bird divan. Top with cheese and bake uncovered at 350°F for 45 minutes.

WHITE SAUCE

2 T. butter
2 T. flour
^{1}/4 tsp. salt
^{1}/8 tsp. pepper
1 cup milk

Melt butter in saucepan over low heat. Quickly blend in flour, salt and pepper. Cook over low heat, stirring constantly until mixture is smooth and bubbly. Remove from heat; stir in milk. Heat to boiling, stirring constantly. Boil and stir for 1 minute.

Bradley A. Flategraff
Gallatin Gateway, MT

UPLAND GAME BIRDS

DOVE COINTREAU

DOVE COINTREAU

12 doves, dressed
1/4 cup flour
1 T. salt
1 T. pepper
4 T. butter
1 to 2 scallions, chopped
1 cup orange juice
1 to 2 oranges, sliced
1 1/2 oz. Cointreau

Mix flour, salt and pepper and roll birds in mixture. Brown birds and scallions in butter, then set aside. Make gravy from drippings. Place birds, gravy, orange juice and orange slices in Dutch oven. Cover and simmer for 1 hour or until done. Just before serving, add Cointreau.

Robert Greggs
Augusta, WV

PERFECT PHEASANTS

2 pheasants, cut up
1/2 cup flour
1 tsp. salt
1 tsp. paprika
1/8 tsp. pepper
1/8 tsp. basil
1/4 cup butter or shortening
1 clove garlic, crushed
1/4 cup ripe olives, chopped
1/2 cup water
1/2 tsp. Worcestershire sauce
1/2 cup white cooking wine

Combine flour, salt, paprika, pepper and basil. Dredge pheasants in flour mixture. Melt butter or shortening in skillet. Add pheasant and garlic; brown pheasant on both sides. Add olives, water and Worcestershire sauce. Cover and simmer for 45 minutes. Turn pheasant and add wine. Simmer 45 minutes more. Add water for extra sauce.

Les Zearing
Bagley, MN

CHAPTER 4

SMALL GAME

H ere is hunting adventure all its own. Maybe the sur-
roundings aren't wilderness—possibly some farmland
around home, a mosaic of brush patches and woodlots and
fields—but the hunt is still exciting, the game a challenge,
and the whole package downright fun.

Fortunately, the fun continues in the kitchen—if you're
armed with the right recipe ideas—and then on the table. So
here are NAHC members' methods for celebrating small
game—squirrel, rabbit and more—that can be as delicious as
anything you've ever created on a stove or in an oven.

The game may be small but the taste can be superb. These
recipes prove it.

*"Evening Creek Farm" by Steven R. Kozar. Courtesy of the artist
and Wild Wings Inc., Lake City, MN 55041. (800) 445-4833.*

Oven-Barbecued Squirrel

2 squirrels, whole or cut up
1 cup chopped onion
1 T. butter
$^1/_2$ cup cider vinegar
$^1/_2$ cup ketchup
3 T. brown sugar, molasses or honey
3 T. bourbon, apple juice or orange juice
1 tsp. dry mustard or 2 tsp. prepared mustard
$^1/_4$ tsp. Tabasco sauce

For barbecue sauce, cook onion in butter in Dutch oven over medium heat until just tender, stirring occasionally. Add all remaining ingredients except squirrel. Heat just to boiling. Reduce heat and simmer about 5 minutes, stirring occasionally. Add squirrels to Dutch oven, turning to coat with sauce. Bake at 350°F for 2 hours or until meat is extremely tender, turning meat occasionally. Remove squirrels from sauce and set aside until cool enough to handle. Pull meat from bones and shred coarsely, discarding bones. Return meat to sauce and reheat on stovetop until heated through. Serve in a sandwich or over hot cooked rice or noodles.

Barbecue sauce may be prepared up to a few days in advance. Entire recipe may be made up to 2 days ahead and refrigerated. Reheat gently over medium-low heat before serving. Meat will become tough if reheated at too high a heat.

Teresa Marrone
Minneapolis, MN

SQUIRREL BOG

2 fox squirrels or 3 gray squirrels, quartered
3 quarts water, approximately
1 1/2 lbs. kielbasa, Italian, venison or other link sausage
3 cups uncooked white rice
Salt and pepper

Cover meat with water and cook in pressure cooker or stock pot until meat readily separates from bones. Strain and save cooking liquid. Debone meat and return to cooking liquid; add sausage and rice. If necessary, add sufficient water to cook rice. Simmer in open pot at a low boil for 30 minutes or until rice is fluffy and tender and all liquid has evaporated or has been absorbed.

Bogs, whether done with fowl, squirrel or other types of meat, are a traditional Southern dish, particularly popular in South Carolina. They offer a wonderful way to marry the flavor of wild game with rice while extending the meat to make more servings.

Jim Casada
Rock Hill, SC

Beans, Beer and Beaver Tail

1 beaver tail
3 cups dried navy beans
6 slices bacon
1 qt. beer
3/4 cup molasses
2$^{1}/_{2}$ tsp. dry mustard
1/4 cup minced onion
1 clove garlic, minced
2 tsp. salt

Skin beaver tail by holding over flame and charring until skin blisters and comes off in sheets. Cube the meat. Place beans in large Dutch oven and cover with cold water and bring to a boil. Boil for 5 minutes, remove from heat and let stand for 1 hour. Drain. Add water to cover beans and bring to a boil. Reduce heat, cover and simmer for 1 hour. Drain, reserving liquid and setting beans aside. Chop 3 slices of bacon and place in bottom of Dutch oven. Mix beans with beaver tail and put in Dutch oven. Mix beer, molasses, mustard, onion, garlic and salt and pour over beans, adding bean liquid if necessary to cover beans. Place 3 slices whole bacon on top, cover and bake at 250°F for 6 to 8 hours. Add bean liquid, beer or water as needed to keep beans barely covered. Remove lid during last hour of cooking to brown beans.

Andi Flanagan
Seward, AK

WATCHAGOT STEW

Wild game
4 (14¹/2-oz.) cans diced tomatoes
1 cup water
2 bay leaves
1 beef bouillon cube
1¹/2 tsp. oregano
3 cloves garlic, chopped
2 tsp. salt
1 tsp. pepper
2 T. sugar
¹/3 cup flour
1 tsp. salt
¹/2 tsp. pepper
2 T. olive oil
2 large onions, chopped
3 large potatoes, cubed
2 ribs celery, chopped
3 large carrots, sliced
3 T. flour

Combine tomatoes, water, bay leaves, bouillon cube, oregano, garlic, salt, pepper and sugar in large, heavy pan. Cover and simmer for 1 hour. Mix flour, salt and pepper and coat 2 cleaned and cut-up rabbits or 3 cleaned and cut-up squirrels or an equivalent amount of quail or dove or 3 pounds cubed wild game or whatever y'got on hand! Brown meat in oil. Add onions and cook for 10 minutes or until tender. Add to simmering tomato mixture and simmer uncovered for about 2 hours or until meat is tender. Add potatoes, celery and carrots to stew and simmer uncovered for 30 to 45 minutes or until vegetables are tender. Mix 3 tablespoons flour with ¹/2 cup cold water and stir until smooth. Add to stew and simmer until slightly thickened. Season to taste with salt and pepper.

Mary Anne Lecce
Collinsville, IL

GAME STIR-FRY

2 cups game meat (animal or fowl), cut into thin strips
3 T. vegetable or olive oil
2 cloves garlic, diced
2 carrots, thinly sliced
1 onion, sliced
2 ribs celery, thinly sliced
1 can water chestnuts, sliced
2 T. cornstarch
1/3 cup sherry
2 t. soy sauce

Heat oil in wok or large skillet. Add meat and garlic; cook quickly, stirring often. Remove meat and set aside. Add carrots, onion, celery and water chestnuts and cook on high, stirring often. After 5 to 10 minutes, when vegetables are cooked but still crisp, return meat to skillet. Combine cornstarch, sherry and soy sauce and add to skillet, stirring constantly until mixture becomes thick and bubbly. Serve hot with cooked rice.

David W. Foxworth
APO AE

SMALL GAME

SQUIRREL STEW

2 squirrels, cleaned and cut into pieces
$1/4$ cup flour
1 tsp. salt
$1/2$ tsp. pepper
2 T. olive oil
3 cloves garlic, minced
2 large onions, chopped
4 cups water
4 beef bouillon cubes
1 large potato, cubed
2 large carrots, diced
2 ribs celery, diced
2 cups frozen lima beans
2 ($14^{1}/2$-oz.) cans diced tomatoes
2 cups frozen corn kernels
1 tsp. Worcestershire sauce
$1^{1}/2$ tsp. sugar
3 T. flour

Dredge squirrel in flour, salt and pepper. Heat olive oil and garlic in large Dutch oven and brown squirrel. Add onions and cook until soft. Add water, bouillon cubes, potato, carrots and celery. Cover and simmer for 1 hour. Add lima beans, tomatoes, corn, Worcestershire and sugar. Cover and simmer for 30 minutes. Mix 3 tablespoons flour with $1/2$ cup cold water, stirring until smooth. Add to stew and simmer until slightly thickened. Season to taste with salt and pepper.

Mary Anne Lecce
Collinsville, IL

SQUIRRELS AND RICE

2 squirrels, cut up
1/2 tsp. salt
1/2 tsp. black pepper
1 bay leaf
1 cup rice, uncooked

Place cut-up squirrel in large pot and cover with water. Add salt, pepper and bay leaf. Bring to a boil and reduce heat. Simmer for 1 to 2 hours or until meat begins to fall off the bone, adding water as necessary. When done, remove bay leaf and discard. Remove squirrel pieces and allow to cool. Remove meat from bones and return meat to pot. Add rice, bring to a boil, reduce heat and simmer for about 30 minutes or until rice is done.

David W. Foxworth
APO AE

White Rabbit Fricassee with Carrot Dumplings

3^1/$_2$ lbs. rabbit, cut into serving pieces
3 T. flour
^{1}/$_3$ cup cold water
1 medium onion, sliced
2 ribs celery, chopped
3 cloves garlic, minced
1 T. salt
^{1}/$_2$ tsp. thyme
^{1}/$_2$ tsp. cracked pepper

Carrot Dumplings
1 cup flour
2 tsp. baking powder
^{1}/$_2$ tsp. salt
3 T. shortening
^{1}/$_2$ cup milk
^{1}/$_4$ cup shredded carrot
1 tsp. dried parsley

Mix flour into water and set aside. Place onion, celery, garlic, salt, thyme and pepper in large Dutch oven and cover with cold water. Bring to a boil, cover and simmer for 2^1/$_2$ to 3 hours or until rabbit is tender. Remove rabbit and cool enough to bone. Add flour mixture to broth and stir over medium heat until lightly thickened. Add rabbit meat and bring to a boil.

To make dumplings: Sift flour, baking powder and salt; cut in shortening. Add milk, carrot and parsley and mix to form dough. Drop into simmering broth in 6 to 8 mounds. Cover and simmer for 15 minutes without lifting lid.

Andi Flanagan
Seward, AK

SMALL GAME

Calamine Rabbit Pie

2 (1½- to 2-lb.) wild rabbits, dressed
4 cups water
1 medium onion, cut into quarters
1 clove garlic, minced
½ tsp. salt
½ tsp. pepper
¼ tsp. cayenne pepper

4 cups ½-inch-cubed red potatoes
2 cups sliced carrots
½ cup sliced celery
½ tsp. dried sage or rosemary
5 cups buttermilk baking mix
1⅔ cups milk
1 T. butter or margarine, melted

Cut up rabbit and combine with water, onion, garlic, salt, pepper and cayenne pepper in 6-quart Dutch oven or stock pot. Bring to a boil over medium-high heat. Reduce heat to low and simmer for 1 to 1½ hours or until meat is tender. Remove from heat and remove rabbit from broth. Cool slightly. Remove meat from bones and discard bones. Return meat to broth. Stir in potatoes, carrots, celery and sage or rosemary. Cook over low heat for 30 to 35 minutes or until broth is reduced by half and vegetables are tender, stirring occasionally. Remove from heat and set aside.

Spray 13 x 9-inch baking dish with vegetable cooking spray. Combine baking mix and milk in medium mixing bowl and stir with fork until soft dough forms. Divide dough in half. On lightly floured surface, roll half of dough into 14 x 10-inch rectangle. Fit into prepared baking dish, pressing dough over bottom and up sides of dish. Spoon meat filling evenly into dough-lined dish.

Roll remaining dough into 13 x 9-inch rectangle and place over filling. Roll edges of bottom and top crusts together. Flute edges or press together with tines of fork to seal. Cut several 1-inch slits in top crust to vent. If desired, in place of top crust, roll crust to ½-inch thickness and cut leaf or rabbit shapes using floured 2- to 3-inch cookie cutters, and arrange on pie, spacing at least 1 inch apart. Bake at 425°F for 20 to 25 minutes or until crust is golden brown. Brush crust with butter or margarine and let pie stand for 5 minutes before serving.

Tom Carpenter
Plymouth, MN

Deep-Fried Rabbit and Pineapple Sandwiches

2 cups chopped, cooked rabbit or ptarmigan
1 cup crushed pineapple, drained
1 cup mayonnaise
16 slices bread
4 eggs, beaten
3 cups vegetable oil
Powdered sugar
Cranberry or currant jelly

Mix rabbit with pineapple and mayonnaise. Spread on 8 slices of bread, top with remaining slices and trim off crusts. Cut each sandwich into 3 parts and dip in beaten egg. Fry in oil heated to 350°F until brown. Drain on brown paper and dust with powdered sugar. Serve with jelly on the side.

Andi Flanagan
Seward, AK

SMALL GAME

PORCUPINE LIVER STICKS

3 porcupine livers
1 bottle Chinese oyster sauce
1 lb. bacon

Soak whole livers in salted water for 15 minutes. Cut livers into thick slices and drop into boiling water for 1 minute. Remove membrane from edges, along with tubes and gristle. Soak in oyster sauce for 10 minutes, then wrap each slice in bacon. Thread onto soaked bamboo sticks or skewers and grill, basting with oyster sauce. A rare and wonderful treat! Porcupine livers are the Cadillac of game livers.

Andi Flanagan
Seward, AK

BRUNSWICK STEW

2 rabbits or 3 squirrels, quartered
3 quarts water, approximately
1 cup butter or margarine
1 pkg. frozen lima beans
1 can tomato chunks
1 pkg. frozen whole-kernel corn
5 potatoes, cubed
1 pkg. frozen okra
Water

Cover meat with water and cook in pressure cooker or stock pot until meat readily separates from bones. Strain and save cooking liquid. Remove meat from bones and return meat to liquid. Add butter, lima beans, tomatoes, corn, potatoes and okra; stir thoroughly. Bring to a boil and simmer for 2 to 3 hours, adding additional water as necessary.

There are many variations on Brunswick stew, a popular Southern dish. If desired, other vegetables or game can be substituted for those given here. Raccoon and muskrat, for example, lend themselves to the making of fine Brunswick stews.

Jim Casada
Rock Hill, SC

WILD GAME PIE

Game bird or meat
1 medium onion, chopped
¹/₂ cup chopped celery
2 cups chopped spinach
1 can cream of mushroom soup
1¹/₂ tsp. curry powder
1 cup chicken stock
   (or beef stock if made with red meat)
2 cups brown rice, cooked
2 cups flour
³/₄ cup cooking oil
1 cup whole wheat flour
¹/₂ cup milk

Simmer onion and raw meat in water until meat is fully cooked. Drain and bone meat and chop. Combine 2 cups meat with onion, celery, spinach, soup, curry powder and chicken stock in large bowl. Cook rice and stir into the mix. Mix regular and whole wheat flours, oil and milk to make crust. Divide dough in half. Place one half between 2 sheets of wax paper and roll out to fit 11-inch diameter deep-dish pie pan. Pour in all filling. Roll remaining half of dough and cover pie plate. Poke lightly with fork and bake at 350°F for about 45 minutes or until crust is cooked.

Lance Goucher
Phoenix, OR

SMALL GAME

RABBIT WITH WINE AND MUSHROOMS

2 lbs. rabbit (or any small game or game
    bird), cut into quarters
Flour
Salt and pepper
2 T. olive oil
1 T. crushed garlic
1 cup chopped onion
2 cups mushrooms, cut into quarters
10-oz. can condensed cream
    of mushroom soup
1 cup water
1 cup red wine

Dust rabbit pieces in flour and salt and pepper to taste. Brown in a hot skillet with olive oil and garlic. When rabbit is browned on all sides, add onion and mushrooms and cook for 2 minutes. Add soup, water and wine, lower heat to a simmer and cook for 1^1/$_2$ hours or until meat is falling off bones. If sauce is too thick, add water or wine to thin.

Dennis L. Morgan
Livonia, NY

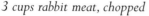

MOOSE PASS CHIMICHANGAS

3 cups rabbit meat, chopped
3 T. butter
1 small onion, diced
1 rib celery, thinly sliced
4 cloves garlic, minced
1 small potato, diced
2 T. flour
3^1/$_2$-oz. can green chile salsa
1 can chicken stock
^{1}/$_2$ tsp. cumin
^{1}/$_2$ tsp. salt
6 large flour tortillas
Oil for deep frying
Shredded lettuce
1 or 2 tomatoes, diced
1 or 2 avocados, diced
Sour cream
Sliced black olives

Sauté rabbit in butter in large skillet for 3 to 4 minutes. Add onion, celery, garlic and potato and cook for another 3 or 4 minutes. Stir in the flour and mix well. Add salsa, stock, cumin and salt. Simmer until sauce is thick and potato is cooked, about 8 minutes. Divide filling among tortillas and fold to enclose filling completely. Secure with toothpicks. Deep fry in oil heated to 350°F until golden brown and crispy, turning once. Drain and serve on lettuce with diced tomatoes and avocados, sour cream and olives.

Andi Flanagan
Seward, AK

RABBIT WITH WINE AND MUSHROOMS

CHAPTER 5

WATERFOWL

❧ ═══════◆═══════ ❧

Y ou can sit in a duck blind for hours, or wait shivering
in a pit for a flock of geese to come sailing in, and never
once think about cooking what you've been shooting or
hope to shoot. But get it in the kitchen and you've got a
challenge: creating a meal that gives justice to the unique-
ness of this fine meat.

Fortunately, NAHC members (through years of perfect-
ing their recipes and creating delicious meals from waterfowl) know how to celebrate the flavors and textures of
duck and goose. If there's ever game where cooking advice
is welcome, this is it.

When you work so hard for your game, it makes sense
to celebrate it deliciously. Here's how.

BREAST OF GOOSE
WITH ROSEMARY MUSHROOM SAUCE

2 goose breasts, about 12 oz. each
1 cup garlic red wine vinegar
^{1}/4 cup diced onion
^{1}/4 cup sliced carrots
^{1}/4 cup sliced celery
8 black peppercorns
1^1/4 cups milk
2 cups white rice, cooked
6 T. olive oil
1 cup thinly sliced mushrooms
1^1/4 cup flour
1 T. dried rosemary
Salt and pepper

Marinate goose breasts in garlic red wine vinegar for 4 to 6 hours. Combine onion, carrots, celery, peppercorns and milk in saucepan. Cover and slowly bring milk mixture to a boil. Remove from heat and set covered pan aside for 30 minutes. Place goose breasts and marinade in shallow roasting pan and cover with foil. Roast at 350°F for 25 to 30 minutes or until done. Turn once during roasting and baste occasionally to ensure meat doesn't dry out. Begin cooking rice according to package directions. Add mushrooms to olive oil in a small saucepan. Cook on low heat for 5 minutes, stirring occasionally, until mushrooms are soft. Add flour and cook for 1 minute, stirring constantly. Pour milk mixture through a strainer into mushroom mixture and mix briskly with a whisk. Crush rosemary and add to saucepan. Slowly bring to a boil, stirring or whisking, and cook until mixture thickens. Simmer for 3 minutes and season to taste with salt and pepper. Serve each goose breast on a bed of hot rice and smothered in rosemary mushroom sauce.

Reuth Faw
Chaska, MN

Adam's Golden Goose

Whole goose, plucked and dressed
1 orange
1 apple
Stuffing
$^1/_2$ cup flour
$^1/_4$ tsp. salt

Singe and remove pin feathers from goose. Wash and dry goose inside and out, making sure cavity is clean. Rinse with lukewarm water, then with cold water. Gash $^1/_4$-inch-deep **X** in whole orange. Core whole apple. Place fruit inside cavity of goose and tie legs to tail. Cover and roast at 500°F for 30 minutes. Remove fruit from cavity and discard; pour off excess fat. When slightly cooled, fill cavity with stuffing and retie legs. Dredge or pat goose with mixture of flour and salt. Roast, uncovered, at 450°F for 30 minutes or until flour is browned. Reduce heat to 300°F and finish baking, allowing 25 minutes per pound. Baste every 10 minutes of final $^1/_2$ hour with 1 cup of lukewarm water. This manner of cooking will eliminate all strong or disagreeable fat.

Sandy Boehler
Fargo, ND

KEN'S WILD GOOSE AND WILD RICE CASSEROLE

Breast of goose
6 cups cooked wild rice
1 cup chopped green onion
$^1/_2$ cup chopped bell pepper
8 oz. sliced mushrooms
2 carrots, shredded
4 T. butter
1 T. garlic powder
1 T. seasoned salt
1 T. seasoned pepper
$^1/_2$ cup dry red wine

Prepare rice according to package directions; set aside. Sauté green onion, bell pepper, mushrooms and carrots in butter. Add vegetables to cooked rice; add garlic powder, seasoned salt and seasoned pepper. Fillet goose breast to $^1/_2$-inch-thick slices and brown for 30 seconds per side in 4 tablespoons butter in hot skillet. Pour half of rice mixture into 9 x 13-inch casserole dish. Arrange goose breasts on rice and cover with remaining rice mixture. Pour wine over mixture. Bake at 350°F for 30 minutes. Serve with green beans, mashed potatoes and dry red wine.

Kenneth W. Fortner
Elizabethton, TN

BAKED DUCK WITH WILD RICE

6 duck breasts (or upland game bird breasts)
2 cups wild rice or brown rice
1 T. butter
Poultry seasoning
Salt and pepper
1 can cream of mushroom or celery soup
8 to 10 strips bacon

Prepare rice according to package directions. Melt butter in skillet, season duck breasts to taste and brown on both sides in skillet. When rice is cooked, mix with cream-style soup and spread in bottom of glass pan. Place browned duck breasts on top of rice and cover with strips of bacon. Bake at 425°F for 30 to 45 minutes or until duck is cooked through.

Gary L. Shruck
Fairwater, WI

WATERFOWL

ITALIAN DUCK NUGGETS

Italian Duck Nuggets

6 breasts of large mallard, pintail
   or similar duck
$^1/_2$ cup cornmeal
$^1/_2$ cup grated Parmesan cheese
2 eggs, beaten
5 cloves garlic
$^1/_2$ cup olive oil
1 bay leaf
$^1/_3$ cup dry white wine
$^1/_3$ cup wine vinegar
Salt and pepper

Mix cornmeal and Parmesan cheese. Cut duck breasts into 1-inch pieces, dip in egg and dredge in cornmeal and Parmesan cheese mixture. Sauté garlic in oil until lightly browned. Add duck, coating on all sides until browned. Add bay leaf, wine and vinegar. Cover and simmer for 20 minutes or until cooked through, stirring occasionally. Season with salt and pepper.

Paul Furnari
Elmira, OR

Mom's Duck

1 small duck
Cooking oil
1 carrot, diced
1 onion, diced
1 rib celery, diced
Vegetable oil spray
1 can chicken broth
White wine

Rinse duck in cold water when thawed. If skinned, rub outside thoroughly with cooking oil. Stuff duck very full with carrot, onion and celery. Spray roaster with vegetable oil spray and place duck and stuffing into roaster. Pour chicken broth and white wine over duck. Keep roaster filled with water. Bake at 325°F or 350°F in covered roaster for about 3 hours. Wood duck requires longer baking time.

Shannon Koshiol
Fort Collins, CO

WATERFOWL

SOUTHERN DUCK

1 large or 2 small ducks (with skin on)
Salt and pepper
Thyme
Basil
Oil
Flour
1 onion, diced
12 carrots, diced
1 turnip, diced
2 ribs celery, diced
1 cup red wine
2 cups chicken stock or broth

Cut duck into pieces with skin on. Season duck pieces with salt, pepper, thyme and basil and brown in oil in large skillet. Remove meat from skillet. Add about 1 tablespoon of flour to liquid in pan to make roux; if necessary, add oil or butter. Add onion, carrots, turnip and celery to roux. Pour in wine and stock. Bring to a boil. Return meat to skillet. Lower heat, cover and simmer for $1^1/_2$ hours. Serve with brown rice or sweet potatoes.

Dave Kulaszewski Sr.
Cleveland, OH

BARBECUED GOOSE OR DUCK

2 to 4 goose breasts or 6 to 8 duck breasts
2 T. instant coffee crystals
2 T. Worcestershire sauce
Favorite barbecue sauce

Place goose or duck breasts in slow cooker and cover with water. Add coffee crystals and Worcestershire sauce. Cook slowly on low setting for 6 hours or more. Drain and shred meat. Mix with barbecue sauce and cook in slow cooker for at least 1 hour. Serve on sandwich buns.

Curtis Johnson
Minneapolis

Duck with Ginger Sauce

4 lbs. duck meat, cut into cubes

2 eggs

$^1/_2$ cup flour

$^1/_4$ cup cornstarch

2 T. water

1 tsp. soy sauce

$^1/_4$ tsp. ginger

2 cups oil

1 tsp. soy sauce

$^3/_4$ cup boiling water

$^1/_4$ cup cider vinegar

$^1/_4$ cup rice vinegar

$^1/_2$ cup sugar

1 T. ketchup

1 T. cornstarch

3 T. cold water

1 T. soy sauce

3 T. chopped candied ginger

Make a batter with eggs, flour, cornstarch, water, soy sauce and ginger. Heat oil. Coat duck cubes in batter and deep fry a few pieces at a time in hot oil. Drain on paper towels and keep warm. Mix boiling water, 1 teaspoon of soy sauce, cider and rice vinegars, sugar and ketchup in saucepan until sugar dissolves. Mix cornstarch, cold water and 1 tablespoon of soy sauce together and add to vinegar mixture. Cook over low heat until thickened, stirring constantly. Add candied ginger and pour over duck. Serve with boiled Chinese noodles and steamed pea pods.

Andi Flanagan
Seward, AK

Slow-Cooked Duck with Spinach

1 or 2 ducks (mallard, teal or other waterfowl)

1 medium onion, quartered

3 to 4 potatoes, quartered

3 to 4 carrots, cut into 1-inch chunks

$15^1/_2$-oz. can spinach

1 cup water

Salt and pepper

Favorite seasonings

Wash and clean duck and place in slow cooker. Add onion, potatoes, carrots, spinach, water and seasonings. Slow cook on low for 8 to 10 hours or until tender.

Gary Barger
Hickman, NE

WILD GOOSE AND WILD RICE SOUP

2 small wild geese, skinned
8 oz. (1 1/3 cups) uncooked wild rice
12 oz. fresh mushrooms, sliced
2 T. butter
1 cup chopped onion
1 cup chopped celery
2 T. instant chicken bouillon granules
3/4 tsp. white pepper
3/4 cup dry white wine

Cook wild rice according to package directions for 30 minutes, until partially cooked; drain liquid and set rice aside. Place geese in 5- to 6-quart stock pot with 7 cups water. Bring to a boil and reduce heat. Cover and simmer for 1 hour or until goose is tender. Remove goose from broth and let stand until cool enough to handle. Skim fat from broth, strain broth and set aside. Remove goose meat from bone. Cut into bite-size pieces. In stock pot, cook mushrooms in butter for 4 to 5 minutes until tender. Add onion and celery. Cover and cook for 5 to 10 minutes until tender. Return broth to pan. Add partially cooked wild rice to broth. Stir in bouillon granules, white pepper and salt to taste. Add 4 cups water and bring to a boil. Reduce heat and simmer, uncovered, for 15 minutes. Stir in goose meat and wine. Heat through and serve.

Mary Anne Lecce
Collinsville, IL

DELICIOUS DUCK

2 mallard ducks, whole or cut into pieces
1/2 cup soy sauce
1 cup apricot, peach or pineapple jam
3 T. sugar
2 T. lemon juice
1 1/2 tsp. ground ginger
1/2 tsp. cinnamon
1/2 tsp. nutmeg
1/2 tsp. allspice
1/4 tsp. thyme
1/4 tsp. garlic salt

Mix soy sauce, jam, sugar, lemon juice, ginger, cinnamon, nutmeg, allspice, thyme and garlic salt. Roll duck in marinade, place bird in glass dish, pouring remaining marinade over duck. Bake at 350°F for 1 1/2 hours or until done, basting several times.

Lloyd Dykstra
Junction City, OR

WILD DUCK AND ORANGE SAUSAGE

1 lb. duck breast meat, finely ground and chilled
4 T. butter
3 T. finely chopped shallots
1 clove garlic, minced
$^1/_2$ cup Grand Marnier
4 strips bacon, minced and chilled
$^1/_2$ tsp. paprika
$^1/_4$ tsp. cayenne pepper
$^1/_4$ tsp. ground coriander
$^1/_4$ tsp. chopped fresh thyme
Pinch chopped fresh sage
1 tsp. coarse ground black pepper
1 tsp. curing salt
Medium hog casings

Sauté shallots and garlic in butter. Add
Grand Marnier and heat until liquid is
reduced by half. Combine duck, bacon,
sautéed shallots, paprika, cayenne pepper,
coriander, thyme, sage, black pepper and
curing salt. Mix thoroughly. Stuff mixture
into hog casings. Smoke sausage lightly and
finish by baking at 350°F until the sausage
reaches internal temperature of 160°F.

Dwayne Spencer
Middletown, PA

WATERFOWL

WILD DUCK AND OYSTER GUMBO

2 ducks, cut into pieces
1 cup cooking oil
1 cup flour
1 large onion, chopped
2 qts. warm water
1 pint oysters
Filé powder
Minced parsley
Minced onion tops
2 T. Tabasco sauce

Make a roux by heating oil in large skillet and blending in flour until it browns. Add onion and sauté. Season ducks well with salt and pepper and fry in roux until oil comes out around edges. Add warm water and cook slowly for about 2 hours or until duck is tender. Add oysters 20 minutes before serving. Add filé powder according to instructions on bottle. Remove from heat and sprinkle with parsley, onion tops and Tabasco sauce. Serve with rice, bread and potato salad.

John Tamborella
Milton, FL

WATERFOWL

PEKING DUCK

3 to 4 lb. duck
5 to 6 T. honey
2 tsp. wine vinegar
2 T. soy sauce
2 to 3 tsp. sherry
1 orange
1 onion

Combine honey, vinegar, soy sauce, sherry, juice of ¹/₂ orange and 3 tablespoons water in saucepan. Bring to a boil, then let cool. Prick skin of duck lightly with sharp fork. Pour several pints of boiling water over duck to soften skin; let dry. Place onion and remaining ¹/₂ orange inside duck. Cook bird at 350°F for 20 minutes per pound, basting frequently with sauce. Lower heat halfway through cooking time. Test for doneness by sticking skewer deep into leg meat. If juice runs clear, duck is done.

Lloyd Dykstra
Junction City, OR

WILD DUCK AND OYSTER GUMBO

Goose with Mashed Potato Stuffing

1 large Canada or other goose
2¹/₂ lbs. potatoes, quartered
¹/₄ cup butter
2 eggs
1¹/₂ tsp. ground sage
1 tsp. caraway seed
Salt and pepper
8 slices bacon
3 cups water

Boil potatoes until tender. Drain and combine with butter and eggs; mash until smooth. Add sage, caraway, salt and pepper to taste. Stuff goose with potato mixture and tie legs together. Pre-heat oven to 450°F. Place goose on rack in roasting pan, breast side down, and roast for 20 minutes. Turn breast side up and roast for another 20 minutes. Salt and pepper goose and lay bacon strips across goose. Reduce oven heat to 325°F. Pour water into roaster and cover. Roast for about 2 hours, depending on size of goose. Let rest for 10 minutes before carving. Serve with braised red cabbage and apples. (For recipe see page 68.)

Andi Flanagan
Seward, AK

Snow Goose Jerky

4 halves snow goose breast
6 oz. soy sauce
³/₄ cup water
1¹/₂ T. brown sugar
¹/₂ T. liquid smoke flavoring
1 T. salt
Dash Worcestershire sauce

Cut breast meat lengthwise in thin strips, about ¹/₈-inch thick. Mix soy sauce, water, brown sugar, liquid smoke flavoring, salt and Worcestershire sauce to make marinade. Place meat in marinade for 10 to 15 minutes. Arrange meat on dehydrator racks and sprinkle with pepper. Dry meat for 48 hours. Or place meat on bread racks, sprinkle with pepper, and bake at 250°F for about 4 hours.

Charles Richards
Los Lunas, NM

ROAST WILD GOOSE

Wild Goose
Salt and pepper
1 apple, cut into large pieces
1 orange, cut into large pieces
1 rib celery, cut into large pieces
1 carrot, cut into large pieces
Onion powder
Garlic powder
3 to 4 cups chopped shallots
2 to 3 cloves garlic, crushed
1 cup port wine
Sliced mushrooms
Beef broth

Salt and pepper inside of goose cavity and stuff with apple, orange, celery and carrot pieces appropriate to size of goose. Season outside of goose with salt, pepper, onion powder and garlic powder. Place goose in roaster with chopped shallots, crushed garlic cloves and port wine. Roast, uncovered, at 425°F for 30 to 45 minutes or until skin is brown. Reduce heat to 350°F, cover goose and continue roasting for 2 to 2³/4 hours until goose is done. Add sliced mushrooms to roaster during the last half hour of cooking. Remove goose from roaster and place under foil tent to keep warm. Degrease pan juices if necessary. Add ¹/2 to 1 cup beef broth to juices in pan, depending on how much gravy you want. Bring to a boil on stove top over medium heat. Thicken gravy with a paste of flour and water, cooking to desired consistency. If desired, season with salt, pepper, garlic powder and onion powder while cooking.

Mary Anne Lecce
Collinsville, IL

WATERFOWL

WORLD'S GREATEST DUCK

World's Greatest Duck

4 skin-on mallard breasts
3 T. sugar
2 T. red wine vinegar
3 T. fresh-squeezed orange juice
2 T. Grand Marnier liqueur
2 T. grated orange rind
1 cup chicken stock
1 T. cornstarch

You'll have to pluck your mallard for this juicy recipe. Fillet duck breasts from bone, leaving skin on. Place breasts on oven-proof tray and bake at 500°F for 7 to 10 minutes or until medium rare. Thinly slice meat diagonally. In a small saucepan, caramelize sugar over low heat and add vinegar, orange juice, Grand Marnier and grated orange rind. Add chicken stock thickened with cornstarch. Spoon sauce over sliced duck and serve with red cabbage, snap peas and wild rice.

Joey Goff
Opelika, AL

Canada Goose Breast Country-Style

¹/2 goose breast, skinned and sliced
    to ¹/4-inch thickness
Flour
4 T. extra virgin olive oil
¹/2 cup sliced portobello mushrooms
Salt and pepper
¹/4 cup port wine
¹/4 cup Madeira wine
1 T. black currant jelly
4 T. brown gravy

Dust sliced goose breast in flour and sauté in olive oil for about 1 minute on each side; be sure not to overcook. Add sliced portobello mushrooms and season with salt and pepper to taste. Add port wine and Madeira wine and allow to flame to burn off alcohol. Add black currant jelly and brown gravy. Simmer for 1 to 2 minutes. Serve over wild rice.

Saul Cenicacelaya
Dover, NJ

WATERFOWL

Index